100 AMAZING FACTS ABOUT THE MAYANS

2024, Marc Dresgui

Index

Introduction 6
Fact 1 - The Mayans invented the concept of zero 7
Fact 2 - The Mayans observed the stars without telescopes 8
Fact 3 - The Mayan pyramids had secret passages 9
Fact 4 - The Maya built cities without wheels 10
Fact 5 - The Mayan calendar was incredibly accurate 11
Fact 6 - The Maya played a ritual ball game 12
Fact 7 - The Mayans accurately predicted eclipses 13
Fact 8 - The Maya built dams to manage water resources 14
Fact 9 - The Mayans farmed on mountain terraces 15
Fact 10 - Mayan white roads cut through the jungle 17
Fact 11 - Mayan temples aligned with the stars 18
Fact 12 - The Maya had sophisticated observatories 19
Fact 13 - The Maya used plants to treat illnesses 20
Fact 14 - The Maya lived in independent city-states 21
Fact 15 - The Mayans wrote with complex hieroglyphs 22
Fact 16 - The Maya worshipped animal gods 23
Fact 17 - The Maya carved jade into sacred objects 24
Fact 18 - The Maya kept precise accounting records 25
Fact 19 - Mayan elites drank spiced cocoa 26
Fact 20 - Jaguars were symbols of power 28
Fact 21 - Seashells were used as currency by the Mayans 29
Fact 22 - Mayan houses withstood tropical conditions 30
Fact 23 - The Mayans followed the cycles of Venus 31
Fact 24 - Mayan languages were diverse and sophisticated 32
Fact 25 - Mayan frescoes told colorful stories 33
Fact 26 - Mayan kings wore extravagant headdresses 34
Fact 27 - The Mayans used calendars to predict the seasons 35
Fact 28 - Mayan hanging gardens fed their cities 36
Fact 29 - The Maya built observation platforms 37
Fact 30 - Mayan warriors used wooden shields 39
Fact 31 - The stelae recounted the exploits of kings 40
Fact 32 - Obsidian jewelry was prized by the Mayans 41
Fact 33 - The Maya celebrated the cycles of the sun 42
Fact 34 - The Maya built sturdy suspension bridges 43
Fact 35 - The Maya carved monumental statues 44
Fact 36 - The Mayans invented games with dice 45
Fact 37 - Natural pigments colored Mayan frescoes 46
Fact 38 - The Mayans believed in a multi-storey world 47
Fact 39 - The Maya used earthbows for their ceremonies 48
Fact 40 - The Maya used conches as instruments 50
Fact 41 - The Maya used steam baths to purify their bodies 51
Fact 42 - The Maya built drainage systems 52
Fact 43 - Ceramic masks were used for ritual purposes 53

Fact 44 - Caves were sacred places for the Mayans 54
Fact 45 - The Maya developed advanced irrigation techniques 55
Fact 46 - Mayan boats were used for maritime trade.................................... 56
Fact 47 - Natural dyes colored their clothes.. 57
Fact 48 - Medicinal gardens were common among the Mayans 58
Fact 49 - Mayan frescoes used to decorate important buildings................... 59
Fact 50 - The cenotes were sacred wells for the Mayas 61
Fact 51 - Mayan ritual dances honored the gods 62
Fact 52 - The Mayans invented underground irrigation systems 63
Fact 53 - The Mayans predicted the weather by observing the sky 64
Fact 54 - Mayan markets were lively and well organized............................... 65
Fact 55 - Mayan cities had different levels and structures............................. 66
Fact 56 - Bone instruments created the music for ceremonies.................... 67
Fact 57 - The Maya wove intricately patterned garments............................. 68
Fact 58 - The Mayans had balanced diets... 69
Fact 59 - Precious stones were used for divination 70
Fact 60 - Masks honored ancestors during ceremonies................................ 72
Fact 61 - Shuffleboard was a Mayan pastime 73
Fact 62 - Rituals marked royal births 74
Fact 63 - Skin drums were part of Mayan ceremonies 75
Fact 64 - Agricultural activities were guided by lunar cycles........................ 76
Fact 65 - Mayan frescoes celebrated great victories 77
Fact 66 - The Maya carved obelisks to make history 78
Fact 67 - The Maya had rare zoos.. 79
Fact 68 - The Maya had food preservation methods 80
Fact 69 - Underground reservoirs used to store water 81
Fact 70 - Royal costumes were adorned with colorful feathers 83
Fact 71 - Mayan rituals for solar eclipses were complex............................... 84
Fact 72 - Mayan pottery was used to store food.. 85
Fact 73 - Mayan temples honored specific gods 86
Fact 74 - The stars were considered sacred guides....................................... 87
Fact 75 - Clay figurines tell ancient myths 88
Fact 76 - Mayan calendars were carved in stone... 89
Fact 77 - Jewelry was used to indicate Mayan social rank 90
Fact 78 - Obelisks commemorate significant events 91
Fact 79 - Shell instruments were used for ritual purposes 92
Fact 80 - The Mayans kept bees to harvest honey 94
Fact 81 - Mayan rituals invoked rain for crops 95
Fact 82 - Animal sculptures represented Mayan gods 96
Fact 83 - Tapestries adorned Mayan royal palaces 97
Fact 84 - The Maya celebrated harvests with special festivals 98
Fact 85 - Bone flutes used to accompany religious rituals 99
Fact 86 - Rituals honored ancestors and spirits 100
Fact 87 - Carved stones recount military exploits.. 101
Fact 88 - Bows and arrows were used for hunting and rituals 102
Fact 89 - Offerings to the rain gods were frequent.. 103
Fact 90 - Mountains were seen as sacred places... 105

Fact 91 - Rituals for lunar eclipses were mysterious 106
Fact 92 - Jade masks were worn for funerals 107
Fact 93 - Rituals protected harvests from disasters 108
Fact 94 - Botanical gardens had rare medicinal plants 109
Fact 95 - Mayan monuments were aligned with the stars 110
Fact 96 - Statues honored Mayan heroes and kings 111
Fact 97 - The drums were made from unique natural materials 112
Fact 98 - The Maya used glyphs to record laws 113
Fact 99 - The Mayans air-conditioned their cities 114
Fact 100 - Caves were seen as gateways to the beyond 116
Conclusion 117
Quiz 118
Answers 121

"In the heart of the forest, the Mayans built cities, not as a conquest of nature, but as a tribute."

- David Freidel

Introduction

Welcome to the fascinating world of the Maya, a civilization that continues to capture our imagination centuries after its heyday. Through this book, you'll discover 100 Amazing Facts that reveal the richness of their culture, their advanced engineering, their profound spirituality and their incredible mastery of science and the arts. The Maya weren't just pyramid builders; they were observers of the cosmos, masters of glyphs and guardians of age-old traditions.

The Maya thrived in the dense jungles of Yucatán, Guatemala, Belize and beyond, creating magnificent cities and networks of roads that linked their centers of power. Their society was complex, with kings, priests, warriors and artisans each playing an essential role in the continuity of their civilization. Through this book, you'll discover how they overcame the challenges of their environment and created a world that celebrated the beauty of nature and cosmic order.

This book invites you to explore subjects as diverse as the secrets of their calendars, the ingenuity of their irrigation systems, and the mysteries of their sacred rites. Each Fact is a gateway to a unique aspect of Mayan life, giving you a better understanding of how they saw the world, how they interacted with their gods and how they left an indelible mark on history.

The Maya have left us a legacy that goes far beyond majestic ruins and carved glyphs. Their understanding of astronomy, sophisticated art and philosophy of time continue to influence our modern world. By diving into these 100 Facts, you can not only admire their ingenuity, but also reflect on how their knowledge and beliefs still resonate today.

Ready to travel through time and space to discover a civilization as brilliant as it is enigmatic? Then turn the page and let yourself be guided by the wisdom and mysteries of the Maya. Let this book be a source of inspiration and discovery for you, a window onto a world where past and present meet in eternal dialogue.

Marc Dresqui

Fact 1 - The Mayans invented the concept of zero

The Maya were one of the first civilizations to use the concept of zero, an innovation that changed the way we do calculations. The zero is represented by a simple shell or empty seed in Mayan writing, demonstrating their ability to create symbols for complex ideas. While other ancient civilizations, such as the Romans, had no number to represent "nothing", the Mayans developed this idea as early as the 3rd century AD. The zero enabled them to make much more precise calculations, notably for their calendars.

The Maya used a vigesimal numbering system, based on the number 20, unlike the decimal system we use today. In this system, the zero played a crucial role in marking positions and values in their calculations. For example, the zero made it possible to distinguish 20 from 200 or 2,000, thus facilitating the manipulation of large numbers in their astronomical calculations. This shows just how advanced their understanding of mathematics was for the time.

The Mayan zero was not just a mathematical concept; it also had cosmic significance. For the Mayans, zero represented the end of one cycle and the beginning of another, a symbol of renewal and continuity. This is reflected in their calendars, where each cycle of time ends with a zero point before beginning again. This use of zero went beyond mathematics and connected deeply with their vision of the world and the universe.

A concrete example of the Maya's use of zero can be found in their complex calendars, such as the Haab and Tzolk'in calendars. These calendars required precise calculations to predict celestial events and rituals. Thanks to the zero, Mayan scribes could mark specific periods without ambiguity. For example, they could accurately indicate that an event would occur after a full 365-day cycle, which would have been impossible without the concept of the zero.

This Mayan mathematical innovation influenced the cultures that followed them, including the Aztecs, and showed just how advanced this civilization was for its time. The concept of zero eventually crossed continents and centuries to become an essential basis of our modern numbering system. Today, even if we use it without thinking about it, it's fascinating to remember that this simple symbol for "nothing" began with an ancient culture, deep in the jungles of Central America.

Fact 2 - The Mayans observed the stars without telescopes

The Maya were passionate astronomers, long before the invention of the telescope. Using only their eyes and simple tools like aligned sticks, they carefully observed the night sky. The Mayans were able to identify the stars and planets, and even track their movement through the seasons. They built their temples and observatories at strategic heights, away from trees and mountains, to get a clear view of the sky. This attention to detail and the environment enabled them to gather precise data on celestial bodies.

One of the Mayans' most impressive feats was their ability to track the movements of the planet Venus. Without a telescope, they observed Venus reappear in the sky after regular 584-day cycles. This observation was not just a scientific curiosity; it was deeply integrated into their calendar and rituals. The Maya believed that the appearances of Venus influenced important events, such as wars or religious rituals. Their precision was so great that it rivaled that of modern astronomers, demonstrating the breadth of their knowledge.

The Maya also observed the phases of the Moon with astonishing accuracy. They not only knew how to identify lunar phases, but also how to predict eclipses. For them, each phase of the Moon had a particular meaning and influenced earthly activities, such as planting or religious ceremonies. The Maya even had names for each phase and celebrated certain moments in the lunar cycle with specific rituals. These meticulous observations were recorded in their codexes, accordion-fold books containing a wealth of astronomical information.

Another example of their mastery of astronomy is the alignment of their buildings with celestial events. At Chichen Itza, one of the most famous Mayan sites, the temple of Kukulcán is aligned in such a way that, during the equinoxes, the Sun casts snake-like shadows down the stairs. This impressive sight, which was no accident, shows the extent to which the Mayans understood the relationship between the Earth, the Sun and the stars. They used these alignments to mark important moments in their ritual calendar.

The Maya also used structures called "E-groups", which are architectural complexes built to track the rising and setting of the Sun at specific times of the year. These structures, found at several Maya sites such as Uaxactun, were rudimentary but effective observatories. They demonstrate how the Maya were able to track the annual cycle of the Sun without any modern equipment.

Fact 3 - The Mayan pyramids had secret passages

Mayan pyramids are not only impressive for their size and architecture; they also conceal fascinating secrets, including hidden passages within their massive structures. These secret passages, often well camouflaged, had many functions, from access routes for priests to shelters for sacred treasures. At the time, these invisible paths were carefully integrated into the design of the pyramids, as a way of protecting what lay inside and maintaining the mystery surrounding Mayan rituals.

One of the most famous discoveries of these secret passages was made at the Kukulcán pyramid in Chichen Itza. Inside this great pyramid, archaeologists discovered a hidden staircase leading to a secret chamber housing a jade-encrusted statue of a red jaguar. This space was not visible from the outside and shows just how careful the Maya were to hide important symbols within their constructions. These passages served not only to protect these objects, but also to symbolically link them to the gods and forces of the universe.

Secret passages in Mayan pyramids could also serve as discreet communication routes between different parts of a temple or ceremonial structure. At Palenque, in the Temple of Inscriptions pyramid, a long hidden staircase leads down to the tomb of King Pakal, a highly respected Mayan ruler. Discovered in the 1950s, this underground access route was carefully sealed after burial, concealing the royal burial site for centuries. These passages were designed not only to ensure respect for the repose of the dead, but also to preserve the mysteries and rituals associated with royal burials.

Some of these secret passages were also used for private religious ceremonies, far from the public eye. Mayan priests and elites used these paths to gain discreet access to the pyramids' inner sanctuaries, where they performed rituals reserved for the initiated. Sometimes, these passages led to secluded chambers where offerings were made to the gods, reinforcing the link between humans and the divine. The Maya believed that these hidden places were points of direct contact with the celestial powers, which is why it was so important to keep these access points secret.

The secret passages bear witness to the great ingenuity of Mayan architects, who were able to combine the monumental beauty of their pyramids with practical and mystical functions. They are a striking example of how the Maya combined their spiritual beliefs with technical know-how.

Fact 4 - The Maya built cities without wheels

The Maya built huge, prosperous cities without ever using the wheel, an essential tool in many other civilizations to facilitate transportation. Yet this absence of wheels did not prevent them from developing complex urban centers, complete with temples, palaces and monumental plazas. Mayan cities such as Tikal and Copán were engineering marvels, built in the middle of dense jungles and on rugged terrain. Their ability to transport heavy building materials over long distances by human power alone remains a fascinating feat.

The absence of the wheel among the Maya can be explained in part by their environment. Maya roads, often called "sacbés", were raised paths paved with white stones, linking different parts of the cities and facilitating transport on foot. In the wet jungles and uneven soils of the Maya region, the wheel would not have been as efficient as on level ground. In addition, the Maya did not use draught animals such as horses or oxen, which further reduced the wheel's usefulness for heavy loads.

To transport heavy stones, such as those used in the construction of their pyramids and palaces, the Maya used wooden sledges and logs. These ingenious techniques enabled them to move massive blocks of stone over great distances. Coordinated teams of workers slid the materials along the logs, much as the Egyptians did for the pyramids. This method required rigorous organization and a large workforce, but it was perfectly suited to their context.

Maya ingenuity was also evident in the construction of their roads. Sacbés were not just footpaths; they were symbols of power and connection between towns. Some of these roads stretched for dozens of kilometers, crossing swamps and rivers, yet remaining functional in all seasons. These roads were built in layers, with a base of stone and gravel, then covered with a white plaster that glistened in the sunlight, making them easy to navigate even at night.

The fact that the Maya were able to build and maintain large cities without the wheel is a testament to their adaptability and mastery of their environment. They knew how to exploit local resources and develop transportation and construction methods that met their specific needs. Mayan cities were dynamic centers, full of activity and life, demonstrating that even without the tools we today consider indispensable, a civilization can reach heights of complexity and grandeur.

Fact 5 - The Mayan calendar was incredibly accurate

The Mayan calendar is one of the most impressive achievements of this civilization, as much for its complexity as for its precision. Unlike our Gregorian calendar, which has a 365.25-day year, the Mayans calculated that the solar year lasted around 365.2420 days. This precision is remarkable, as it comes very close to the exact length of the Earth's year as measured today with our modern technologies. The Mayans achieved this feat without the sophisticated astronomical tools we have today, thanks solely to meticulous observations of the sky over several centuries.

The Maya used two main calendars to manage their daily life and rituals: the Haab and the Tzolk'in. The Haab, which most closely resembles our calendar, consisted of 18 months of 20 days each, plus a short period of 5 days, making a total of 365 days. The Tzolk'in, on the other hand, was a 260-day ritual calendar used to plan religious and ceremonial events. These two calendars worked in tandem, forming a longer cycle called the "Calendar Round", which was repeated every 52 years.

The long calendar, another Mayan innovation, was used to record dates over very long periods. Unlike the short cycles of the Haab and Tzolk'in, the long calendar could count years over millennia, enabling the Maya to mark historical or prophetic events with great precision. This system was based on a countdown of days from a fixed starting date, 3114 BC according to our own calendar. Thanks to this calendar, the Maya were able to date events well beyond their own time.

The Maya used their calendars for much more than simply keeping track of time. They used them to predict astronomical events, such as eclipses or planetary movements, which were of great importance in their culture. Calendar dates were also used to determine the best times to plant crops, organize wars or perform religious rituals. For example, key dates for sacrifices or important ceremonies were often chosen according to their correspondence with specific Tzolk'in days.

The influence of the Mayan calendar extended far beyond the borders of their civilization, affecting other Mesoamerican cultures that adopted elements of this system. The precision of their calendars bears witness to their incredible understanding of time and the universe, rooted in their daily lives and spirituality.

Fact 6 - The Maya played a ritual ball game

For the Maya, the ball game was much more than just a sport; it was a sacred ritual symbolizing the struggle between the forces of good and evil, life and death. This game, known as "Pok-ta-Pok" or "pitz", was played on specially designed fields, often located in the center of towns, such as Chichen Itza or Copán. These fields, known as "ball playing fields", were lined with sloping walls with stone rings fixed high up. The object of the game was to pass a heavy rubber ball through these rings, but only using the hips, elbows and knees.

The ball used in this game was made of solid rubber and could weigh several kilograms, making it difficult to handle. Players had to show great skill and strength to control the ball without using their hands or feet. This physical challenge reflected the importance of the game to the Maya: it was not only a demonstration of athletic prowess, but also a means of winning the honor of the gods. Players wore leather protectors to avoid injury, as the ball could inflict painful blows.

Ball games often had symbolic and religious significance. The Maya believed that the game reflected the movement of the stars and planets, and each game could represent important cosmic events. In some versions of Mayan myth, the game of ball was linked to the story of twin heroes who confronted the lords of the underworld in a game decisive for the fate of the world. These legendary tales inspired players and spectators alike, who saw each match as a rehearsal for celestial battles.

Competition was not only entertainment, it could also be a matter of life and death. In some cases, the losers of a ball game were sacrificed to the gods, a practice that reinforced the ritual and sacred aspect of the sport. This possibility of sacrifice showed that the game of ball went far beyond mere pleasure or competition; it was an act deeply linked to Mayan religion and cosmology. The winners, for their part, could receive honours or riches, testifying to the importance of this game in Mayan society.

Ball courts are still visible today at many archaeological sites, testifying to their central role in Mayan culture. Their walls are often adorned with sculptures depicting players, gods and game scenes, reminding us just how integral this sport was to their daily and spiritual lives.

Fact 7 - The Mayans accurately predicted eclipses

The Maya possessed an impressive knowledge of astronomy, enabling them to predict complex celestial events, such as solar and lunar eclipses, with great accuracy. They carefully observed the sky and recorded the cycles of the stars over long periods, using complex calendars to spot recurring patterns. Their ability to predict eclipses was not just a scientific feat; it also had profound religious and cultural significance. The Maya saw these phenomena as important signs from the gods, directly influencing earthly events.

To calculate eclipses, the Maya used their long calendar, combined with specific cycles called "eclipse series". These series were detailed records of when the Sun and Moon appeared to align in a way that caused an eclipse. Thanks to repeated observations and meticulous calculations, the Maya were able to predict when the next eclipse would occur, sometimes years in advance. This precision demonstrates their ability to understand and quantify complex cycles that eluded other civilizations of the time.

A striking example of their knowledge is the famous Table of Eclipses, found in the Dresden Codex, one of the few surviving Mayan books. This table contains calculations for 11,960 days, or around 33 years, and accurately predicts lunar and solar eclipses. This document proves that the Maya knew not only how to predict eclipse dates, but also how to understand their frequency and duration. Their ability to create such a table testifies to the importance they attached to celestial events and their central place in Mayan society.

Eclipse predictions played a crucial role in the planning of ritual and political events. An eclipse could be seen as a favorable or unfavorable omen, influencing decisions such as the launch of a war or the appointment of a king. Astronomical priests, who possessed the knowledge to interpret these signs, occupied a highly respected place in the Maya hierarchy. When an eclipse was forecast, specific rituals were organized to appease the gods, as an eclipse, especially a solar one, was often seen as a battle between the forces of day and night.

The Maya also built specific structures for observing celestial phenomena, such as "E-groups", aligned to facilitate observation of solstices, equinoxes and eclipses. These buildings, often placed high up, offered an unobstructed view of the horizon, enabling priests to follow the movement of the Sun, Moon and stars.

Fact 8 - The Maya built dams to manage water resources

The Maya lived in regions where access to water was a constant challenge, especially during the dry season. To meet this vital need, they developed ingenious systems to capture, store and manage water. Among these innovations, the construction of dams was one of the most remarkable solutions. These dams were not simply structures to hold back water; they were part of a complex water management network, including reservoirs, canals and cisterns. Their ability to design such systems testifies to their advanced understanding of hydrology.

A striking example of this ingenuity can be found at Tikal, a great Mayan city deep in the Guatemalan jungle. Tikal had no permanent rivers, and natural springs were scarce. To overcome this problem, the Maya built several dams to create artificial reservoirs. These reservoirs, called "aguadas", collected rainwater and held it back for dry periods. The dams, made of stones and compacted earth, controlled the flow of water and prevented flooding during the rainy season.

Maya dams were not only used to supply water for daily consumption, but also to irrigate crops. Farmland was often located close to reservoirs, allowing efficient water distribution for fields of corn, beans and squash, crops essential to the Mayan diet. By using dams to manage water, the Maya were able to maintain high agricultural yields even in times of drought, ensuring the survival of their communities.

At Palenque, another Mayan city, archaeologists discovered a complex dam that not only controlled water, but also created sufficient pressure to power a fountain, one of the first known in the New World. This water management system demonstrates not only the technical ingenuity of the Maya, but also their concern to improve the quality of life by integrating elements of comfort into their cities. The Palenque dam illustrates the extent to which the Maya were able to combine utility and aesthetics in their constructions.

These dams were essential to the prosperity and growth of the great Mayan cities, which could house tens of thousands of people. Water management was a matter of survival and power, and those who mastered this element could exert great influence on their society.

Fact 9 - The Mayans farmed on mountain terraces

The Maya were experts in agriculture, adapting to difficult terrain to feed their people. In mountainous regions, they developed an ingenious system of terraced farming to maximize the use of sloping land. These terraces were built into the hillside, supported by stone or earthen walls, which prevented erosion and retained rainwater. Thanks to this technique, the Maya were able to cultivate fields even in steep and often arid areas, making these otherwise unusable soils productive and fertile.

Through the use of terraces, the Maya were able to control the irrigation of their crops. By strategically placing the terraces, water flowed gently from one level to the next, infiltrating the soil at every stage. This system not only conserved water during the dry season, but also reduced the risk of flooding during the rainy season. The terraces thus made farming more reliable, even in unpredictable weather conditions, and ensured regular harvests to feed their cities.

The main crops grown on these terraces included corn, beans and squash, the three essential elements of the Mayan diet. These plants were often cultivated together according to the milpa principle, where each plant benefited from the others: maize acted as a stake for climbing beans, and the broad leaves of squash covered the soil to conserve moisture and limit weeds. The terraces also made it possible to diversify crops, by varying the orientation and exposure of the landings to grow different plants according to their needs for sun and water.

The use of terraces was not limited to the mountains of Guatemala or Chiapas, but also extended to the highlands of Yucatán, where the Maya adapted this technique to rocky terrain. There, they used the terraces to create gardens and orchards, growing fruit trees and medicinal plants. This agricultural know-how made it possible to create favorable microclimates for each type of crop, optimizing heat and humidity, demonstrating a deep understanding of the interactions between plants and their environment.

The Maya's agricultural terraces bear witness to their ability to transform their environment in a sustainable and ingenious way. These constructions not only served to feed the population, but were also an integral part of landscape management, reducing ecological impact while increasing productivity.

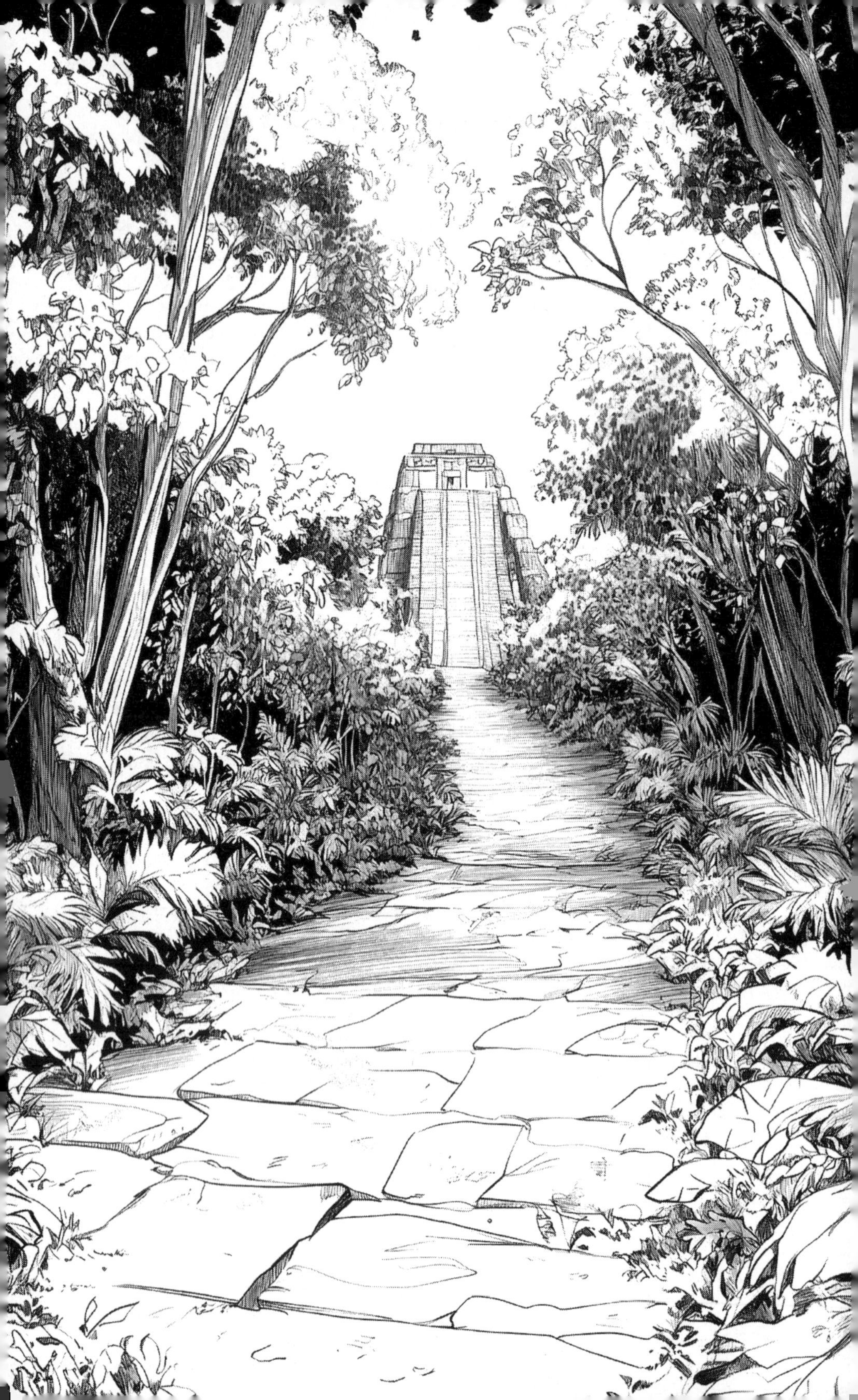

Fact 10 - Mayan white roads cut through the jungle

The Maya built an impressive network of roads called "sacbés", which means "white roads" in the Mayan language. These roads were covered with crushed limestone stones which, once compacted and bleached by the sun, shone brightly in the jungle. These roads were not only utilitarian; they also symbolized important connections between cities, ceremonial centers and surrounding regions. Sacbés were often raised and paved, making travel easier in the rugged, swampy terrain of the Yucatán Peninsula and other Maya regions.

One of the most remarkable roads is the sacbé linking the cities of Coba and Yaxuna, stretching for over 100 kilometers. This road, built through dense jungle, is a testament to the Maya's organization and ability to undertake massive engineering works. The Coba sacbé is not only long, it's also very wide, sometimes measuring up to 10 metres across. Building such roads required meticulous planning and a great deal of manpower to cut the vegetation, lay the foundations and keep the surface white and passable.

The white roads of the Maya served many purposes. They facilitated trade, enabling the transport of goods such as corn, cocoa and other essential agricultural products between cities. They were also communication routes for messengers, who carried important news from one city to another. In a civilization where distance could be a major obstacle, sacbes helped maintain the political and social unity of the various Mayan city-states, contributing to their cultural cohesion.

Sacbés also had a spiritual and symbolic dimension. For the Maya, these roads represented sacred paths linking the terrestrial and celestial worlds. The white roads often led to the main temples and religious centers, facilitating processions and rituals. In Uxmal, for example, the sacbés converge on the Pyramid of the Soothsayer, underlining the importance of this sacred site. The Maya saw these roads as direct links between sacred places, rulers and gods, adding a mystical dimension to their practical function.

These roads are a lasting testimony to the Maya's ability to master and organize their environment. Despite the challenges imposed by thick jungle and difficult terrain, the Maya succeeded in creating a communication and transportation network that rivaled those of contemporary civilizations.

Fact 11 - Mayan temples aligned with the stars

The Maya attached particular importance to the stars, and this fascination was reflected in the precise alignment of their temples with the stars, planets and celestial events. These alignments were not the result of chance, but of meticulous astronomical observation. The Maya used their knowledge to orient buildings to coincide with phenomena such as solstices, equinoxes and planetary movements. This practice strengthened the link between the earth and the cosmos, enabling temples to serve as points of connection between the human world and divine forces.

A striking example of this astronomical alignment can be found at Uxmal, in the Pyramid of the Soothsayer. This temple is oriented so as to align its summit with Venus at certain times of the year. For the Maya, Venus was not only a planet, but also a symbol of the god Kukulcán, associated with war and regeneration. This alignment enabled priests to plan rituals in sync with Venus' appearances in the sky, reinforcing the symbolic power of the temple and the ceremonies held there.

In Chichen Itza, one of the Maya's most famous sites, the temple of Kukulcán offers an impressive spectacle during the equinoxes. At these precise moments, the sun casts shadows that create the illusion of a snake descending the steps of the pyramid, symbolizing Kukulcán itself. This visual effect, carefully crafted by the Maya builders, demonstrates their mastery of architectural alignment and their ability to integrate celestial events into the design of their monuments. This precise alignment shows how the Maya used architecture to bring their myths and beliefs to life.

Mayan temple alignments also served to mark time and the seasons, helping to regulate agricultural and ritual calendars. In the observatory complex at Copán, for example, structures are oriented to mark the solstices and equinoxes, signaling key times for sowing and harvesting. Using the alignments of the stars and the Sun, priests were able to determine propitious periods for agricultural activities, thus ensuring the survival and prosperity of the cities. These alignments demonstrate that for the Maya, heaven and earth were intimately linked, each influencing daily life.

The star-aligned temples are living testimony to Mayan expertise in astronomy and architecture. They illustrate how this civilization was able to integrate its spiritual beliefs and scientific knowledge in constructions that defy time.

Fact 12 - The Maya had sophisticated observatories

The Maya were passionate astronomers, and their interest in the heavens was reflected in the construction of sophisticated observatories. These structures were specially designed to study the movements of the stars, planets and phases of the Moon. Unlike simple buildings, Mayan observatories were often circular or elevated, offering a clear view of the horizon. One of the most famous is the observatory at Chichen Itza, known as El Caracol, which means "the snail" in Spanish, due to its internal spiral staircase.

El Caracol is particularly remarkable for its orientation: it is aligned with the positions of Venus at certain times of the year. The Maya closely followed this planet, which was of great religious and symbolic importance to them. The observatory's windows are positioned to enable the astronomical priests to spot Venus at sunrise and sunset. This attention to detail shows the extent to which the Maya were able to link their terrestrial constructions to celestial movements.

Mayan observatories weren't just used to observe Venus. At Uxmal, another Mayan city, the observatory is oriented to mark the solstices and equinoxes, signaling crucial moments in the agricultural and religious calendars. Priests used these events to organize rituals and ceremonies, aligning human actions with the cosmic calendar. The observatory was also used to calculate lunar cycles, essential for predicting eclipses, as discussed in another Fact in this book.

Mayan observatories were often integrated into temple complexes, showing that astronomy was an essential part of religious and political life. At Copán, for example, priests used the observatory to monitor the movements of the Sun and Moon, helping them to maintain precise calendars. These calendars governed not only agricultural cycles, but also ceremonial activities and festivals, synchronizing city life with the rhythms of the universe. This integration shows the extent to which the Maya saw the heavens as an extension of their terrestrial world.

The use of these observatories demonstrates the technological and scientific advance of the Maya. They lacked modern instruments such as telescopes, but compensated with a deep understanding of natural cycles and ingenious architectural tools. Observatories still stand today, testifying to the Maya's extraordinary know-how and ongoing quest to understand the cosmos. These structures, often located on hills or elevated platforms, enabled the Maya to peer into the sky with a precision that continues to impress modern astronomers.

Fact 13 - The Maya used plants to treat illnesses

The Maya had an in-depth knowledge of plants and their medicinal properties, which they used to treat various illnesses and injuries. Their botanical knowledge was passed down from generation to generation by priests and healers, who played an essential role in the community. The Maya lived in harmony with nature, and their lush environment provided them with a vast natural pharmacy. They knew how to identify which plants could be used to treat common ailments, such as infections, pain or even digestive disorders.

Among the most commonly used plants is ceiba bark, a tree sacred to the Mayans, which was used to prepare infusions to combat fever and pain. The plant's leaves were also used in poultices to soothe inflammation. Another commonly used plant was copal, a resin extracted from trees that was used not only in rituals, but also for its antiseptic properties. Copal was often burned to purify the air and ward off disease, as the Maya believed that the sacred fumes could ward off the evil spirits associated with illness.

The Mayans also used aloe vera for its healing properties. In the event of burns or cuts, healers would apply the gel extracted from aloe leaves directly to the skin to speed healing. This plant, which grows abundantly in hot, arid regions, was a versatile remedy in the Mayan pharmacopoeia. They also used plants such as chamomile to soothe upset stomachs and promote sleep. These treatments, based on empirical knowledge, demonstrate the effectiveness of plants in their healing system.

The Maya didn't just treat symptoms; they sought to balance body and mind by using plants as an integral part of healing rituals. The priests, or "ah men", who served as physicians, saw illness as an imbalance between man and natural forces. Thus, they combined the use of plants with prayers, chants and sometimes offerings to the gods to restore balance and health to the sick. This blend of medicine and spirituality reflected their holistic vision of health.

Mayan knowledge of medicinal plants is still partly used today, particularly by traditional healers in indigenous Central American communities. This ancient knowledge, based on careful observation of nature and repeated experiments, bears witness to the importance of biodiversity to the survival and well-being of the Maya.

Fact 14 - The Maya lived in independent city-states

The Maya did not form a unified empire like the Romans or Aztecs, but rather lived in independent city-states, each with its own government, rulers and cultural idiosyncrasies. These city-states, such as Tikal, Palenque, Calakmul and Copán, were often centered around large plazas and majestic temples, and could be home to thousands of inhabitants. Each city was ruled by a king or queen, often considered an intermediary between the gods and the people, and his or her authority was supported by an elite of priests and nobles.

Each Mayan city-state operated autonomously, with its own laws, rituals and management systems. This meant that relations between cities could be complex, ranging from cooperation and trade to rivalry and war. For example, Tikal and Calakmul, two of the most powerful cities, were in constant competition for control of trade routes and political influence in the region. This rivalry led to strategic alliances and military conflicts, sometimes turning the Yucatán jungles into battlefields.

The Maya city-states were linked by a complex network of roads, such as the sacbés, which facilitated trade and the movement of messengers. Trade was crucial to the economy of the cities, with exchanges of jade, cocoa, textiles and other precious goods. Markets, held regularly in each city, were lively places where inhabitants could buy local and exotic products. This interconnection between cities also enabled the spread of ideas, architectural styles and religious practices, while respecting the independence of each city.

Despite their independence, the Mayan city-states shared a common language, writing systems and similar religious beliefs. They worshipped the same gods, such as the rain god Chaac or the feathered serpent Kukulcán, and followed complex calendars to organize their ceremonies and rituals. This cultural unity ensured a certain cohesion within the Maya civilization, even if each city remained jealous of its political and military autonomy.

The structure of independent city-states shaped the development of Mayan civilization, encouraging innovation, diversity and resilience. Each city could prosper or decline according to its own decisions and its relations with its neighbors. This organizational model enabled the Maya to adapt to a variety of environments, from the mountains of Chiapas to the plains of Yucatán, while leaving a lasting imprint on the region's history and architecture.

Fact 15 - The Mayans wrote with complex hieroglyphs

The Maya had developed one of the most sophisticated writing systems in the ancient world, using complex hieroglyphics to document their history, beliefs and daily life. These hieroglyphs were not simple drawings, but a set of symbols representing sounds, words or concepts. Thanks to this writing, the Maya were able to record precise information on historical events, religious rituals, calendars and even royal dynasties. Their writing was used on stelae, temple walls, ceramics and folded books known as codices.

Mayan hieroglyphs were beautiful and often colorful, carefully carved by highly skilled scribes. Each glyph was a complex combination of geometric shapes, animal images or figures, and could be read in different directions depending on the arrangement of the symbols. Mayan scribes enjoyed a special status in society, as their knowledge enabled them to preserve and pass on knowledge through the generations. They used brushes made from animal hair and natural inks to write on tree bark, creating precious and fragile documents.

One of the best-known examples of Mayan writing is the Dresden Codex, an ancient book containing precise astronomical calculations, including Venus cycles and eclipses. This codex demonstrates the use of hieroglyphs for scientific purposes, but also their role in predicting celestial events that were essential to the planning of rituals and the religious life of the Maya. Hieroglyphics not only conveyed words, but also the cosmological thought and spiritual values of this civilization.

Hieroglyphic inscriptions are also found on stone monuments, where they commemorate the achievements of kings and queens, military victories or political alliances. At Palenque, for example, the Temple of Inscriptions bears a long series of hieroglyphs recounting the exploits of King Pakal the Great. These texts reveal not only the key events of the period, but also the way in which the Maya perceived their world, linking the divine to the mundane through a deeply symbolic script.

The rediscovery and deciphering of Mayan hieroglyphs during the 20th century revealed much about the history and culture of this long-mysterious civilization. This process has shown that the Maya possessed a phonetic script capable of representing complex sounds and words, a rare feat for writing systems of the time.

Fact 16 - The Maya worshipped animal gods

The Maya worshipped a multitude of gods, many of whom took animal forms or combined human and animal traits. This representation reflected their worldview, in which animals were not simply creatures, but embodiments of natural forces and divine aspects. Among these gods, the jaguar held a special place. Associated with night, royalty and power, the jaguar god was venerated as a protector and symbol of strength. Mayan kings, eager to associate themselves with this power, often wore jaguar-shaped ornaments during ceremonies.

Another animal god venerated by the Maya was Kukulcán, the feathered serpent, who represented wind, rain and fertility. Able to slither through any environment, snakes were seen as mediators between the terrestrial and celestial worlds. At Chichen Itza, the temple of Kukulcán is built in such a way as to create the illusion of a snake descending the steps during the equinoxes, recalling the direct link between this god and the movement of the stars. Kukulcán also symbolized wisdom and transformation, qualities that the Maya aspired to integrate into their daily lives.

The Maya also worshipped deities such as Chaac, the god of rain, often depicted with frog or fish features, animals associated with water. In a region where rain was vital for the harvest, Chaac played a central role in agricultural rituals. Priests organized ceremonies to invoke Chaac, using masks and costumes decorated with aquatic motifs, in the hope of provoking beneficial rains. Temples dedicated to Chaac were often decorated with water symbols, illustrating the importance of this divinity to the survival of communities.

Birds, notably the quetzal, also occupied a special place in the Mayan pantheon. The quetzal, with its bright green feathers, symbolized freedom and a link with the heavens. This beautiful bird was associated with nobility and wealth, and its feathers were used to decorate the headdresses of kings and priests. The Maya believed that the gods sometimes communicated in the form of birds, carrying messages between the mortal world and that of the deities. These beliefs reinforced the respect and protection accorded to these creatures.

Respect for animals in Mayan religion went beyond simple veneration; it encompassed a profound understanding of their role in the balance of nature. Each animal was seen as a guardian or guide, endowed with specific qualities that could influence the lives of humans. By attributing divine traits to animals, the Maya recognized the power of nature and its impact on their existence.

Fact 17 - The Maya carved jade into sacred objects

Jade occupied a central place in Mayan culture, not only for its beauty but also for its spiritual and symbolic value. The Maya saw jade as a sacred material, associated with life, fertility and immortality. They used this precious stone to create ritual objects, jewelry and funeral ornaments, reserved for the elite and royalty. Jade, with its deep green color and brilliant reflections, represented renewal and vital energy, qualities highly revered in Mayan society.

Maya craftsmen were extremely skilled at working with jade, despite the stone's hardness, which made carving difficult and required specialized tools. They used sophisticated techniques, such as polishing with sand or other natural abrasives, to shape jade into amulets, funerary masks and other symbolic objects. One of the most famous examples is the funerary mask of King Pakal, discovered at Palenque, which is made of multiple pieces of jade finely fitted to represent the face of the deceased king. This mask illustrates not only the technical expertise of the craftsmen, but also the importance of jade in afterlife rituals.

Jade was not only used in funeral rituals. The Maya also carved pendants, necklaces and earrings, often adorned with symbols and glyphs representing gods or sacred animals. These jewels were not just ornaments, but carried profound meanings and served as protective talismans. Wearing jade was a privilege reserved for the upper classes, and these objects were often handed down from generation to generation, strengthening family and spiritual ties.

Jade's rarity made it a particularly precious material. Jade deposits were located far from the main Mayan cities, in mountainous regions that were difficult to access. This meant that each piece of jade transported and carved represented a considerable effort in terms of trade and logistics. Jade objects were therefore not only symbols of spiritual power, but also of wealth and political influence. Jade exchanges could strengthen alliances between cities or important trading relationships.

Jade objects found in Mayan archaeological sites continue to amaze researchers with their complexity and beauty. These artifacts reveal not only the artistic mastery of the Maya, but also their profound connection with nature and the divine. Each sculpture, polished to perfection, tells a story of belief, power and respect for a material that, for the Maya, captured the very essence of life.

Fact 18 - The Maya kept precise accounting records

The Maya were not only talented builders and astronomers; they also excelled at managing their resources through precise accounting records. They used their advanced numerical system, based on the number zero, to record economic data such as tribute, trade and food stocks. Accounting scribes, who played an essential role in city-states, recorded this information on stone tablets, temple walls or folded codices. These registers made it possible to monitor the city's economy, anticipate needs and ensure the prosperity of the population.

Inscriptions found on stelae and in codices reveal how the Maya tracked tribute payments in corn, cocoa, cloth or precious objects. At Copán, for example, the walls of certain buildings feature hieroglyphs indicating the quantities of goods delivered by tributary villages. These registers served not only to record wealth, but also to reinforce the power of the rulers, who could thus demonstrate their ability to control resources and redistribute goods for the well-being of the city.

The administration of the lively and varied Mayan markets also relied on these accounting records. Markets were essential trading places for local and imported products, such as jade, quetzal feathers and ceramics. Scribes took care to record important transactions, enabling efficient management of taxes and rights of passage. These accounting records provided an overview of economic flows and helped to plan long-term exchanges, guaranteeing stable supplies for the cities.

The Maya also kept accounting records to organize major construction projects, such as pyramids and temples. They noted the quantities of materials required, the teams of workers mobilized and the food rations to be distributed to the workers. At Palenque, for example, inscriptions show how rulers managed resources to build the imposing structures that characterize the city. These documents reveal a rigorous organization and an ability to coordinate vast projects with precision, linking the economic, social and religious aspects of Mayan life.

Although complex and sometimes difficult to decipher, Mayan accounting records testify to the efficiency of their administration and their ability to maintain control over all their city-states. They demonstrate that the Maya possessed a keen sense of management and planning that went far beyond simple calculations.

Fact 19 - Mayan elites drank spiced cocoa

Cacao held a special place in Mayan culture, far beyond its use as a simple food. For the Mayan elite, cocoa was a symbol of wealth, power and divinity. It was consumed as a spicy drink, reserved for kings, nobles and priests at important ceremonies and banquets. This drink was not sweetened like the chocolate we know today, but bitter and spiced with chillies, vanilla and other spices. The Mayans believed that cocoa was a gift from the gods, possessing energetic and even mystical properties.

The Mayans prepared cocoa by grinding cocoa beans into a paste, which they then mixed with hot water. They added spices like chili, which gave the drink a uniquely piquant taste, and ingredients like ground corn to thicken the mixture. The drink was often poured from one container to another to create a froth, considered the most precious and pleasurable part of the beverage. Representations of this preparation can be found in Mayan art, notably on pottery decorated with scenes from court life.

Drinking spiced cocoa was a privilege strictly reserved for the upper classes, and was consumed during rituals and ceremonies in which cocoa played a central role. At royal weddings, for example, cocoa was used to seal unions, and at funeral rites, it accompanied the deceased into the afterlife, symbolizing their elevated status. Cocoa offerings were also made to the gods, and it was sometimes used as currency, illustrating its immense value in Mayan society.

The importance of cocoa went beyond its gustatory pleasure; it was an integral part of traditional Mayan medicine. The drink was believed to heal ailments, restore vigor and even aid concentration for priests and scribes. These virtues attributed to cocoa reinforced its sacred status and made it indispensable in the lives of the elite. Ceremonies involving cocoa were often accompanied by song and prayer, reinforcing its role as a direct link with the divine.

Archaeological discoveries of ceramic vessels bearing cocoa residues have confirmed the importance of this beverage in Mayan life. These vases, often decorated with sophisticated motifs and glyphs describing their contents, were found in the tombs of kings and nobles, testifying to the high esteem in which this beverage was held. Spiced cocoa was much more than a simple delicacy; it represented the quintessence of refinement and spirituality in Mayan civilization, and its consumption was a ritual rich in meaning, linking the elite to their ancestors and the gods.

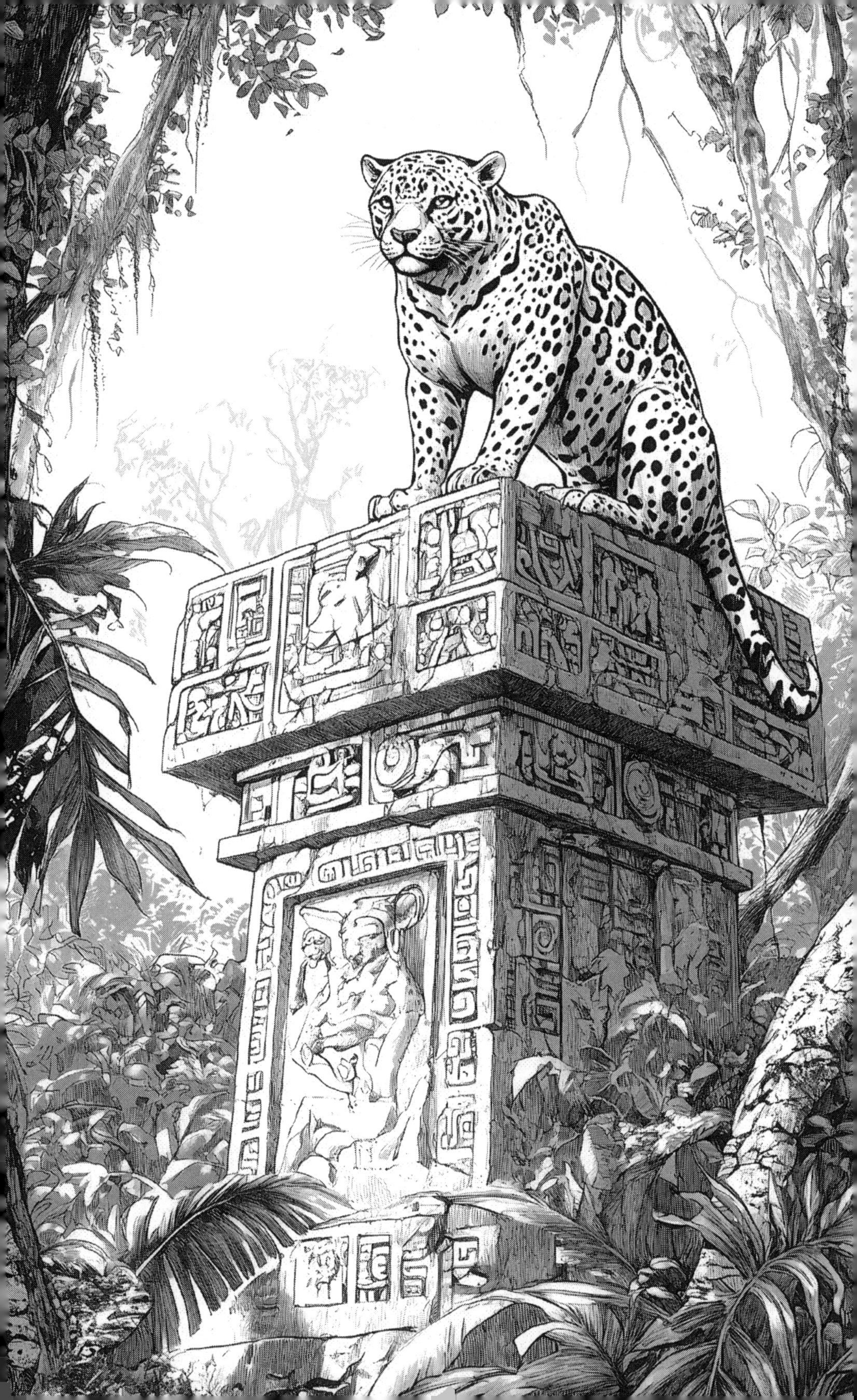

Fact 20 - Jaguars were symbols of power

The jaguar held a prominent place in Mayan culture, representing power, royalty and the spirit world. This majestic animal, with its mottled coat and formidable strength, was considered the embodiment of brute force and divine authority. For the Maya, the jaguar was not simply a feared predator of the jungle, but a sacred being, capable of crossing the boundaries between the world of the living and that of the dead. It also symbolized the night and the power of kings, who sought to appropriate its qualities by wearing jaguar skins or ornaments representing the animal.

Mayan kings and warriors, in their quest for legitimacy and power, often identified with the jaguar. They bore names and titles associated with the animal, such as King Pakal of Palenque, who was often depicted surrounded by jaguar symbols. Jaguars also featured in mythological accounts, where they were depicted as protectors of the gods and guides to the underworld. In sculptures and wall paintings, jaguars are frequently depicted alongside sovereigns, underlining their role as protectors and guarantors of cosmic order.

The jaguar was also associated with the nocturnal sun god, who traveled through the underworld at night before being reborn each morning. This association reinforced the idea that the jaguar possessed supernatural powers, capable of defying death and reigning over dark forces. In ceremonies, priests wore jaguar masks and costumes to invoke these powers and channel the feline's energy into their rituals. These elaborate costumes, adorned with feathers and precious stones, were as much status symbols as they were means of attracting the jaguar's protection.

Elite warriors, known as "jaguar warriors", donned jaguar skins in battle, hoping to capture the animal's ferocity and agility. These warriors were highly respected and played a crucial role in conflicts between city-states. Their bravery and strength were directly associated with the spirit of the jaguar, making them not only formidable fighters, but also semi-divine figures on the battlefield. Wearing the jaguar emblem meant that the warrior was ready to protect his city with the same determination and ferocity as the sacred animal.

Representations of jaguars can be found everywhere in Maya architecture and art, from carved thrones to decorated vases and commemorative stelae.

Fact 21 - Seashells were used as currency by the Mayans

Among the Maya, shells were not only objects of beauty or decorative accessories; they were also used as currency. Shells, especially those from remote coasts, were highly prized for their rarity and brilliance. The most prized were Spondylus shells, vibrant red or deep pink, symbolizing wealth and power. They were used to trade luxury goods such as cocoa, jade and quetzal feathers, essential commodities in the economy of the Mayan city-states.

Shells were incorporated into necklaces or bracelets, and could be used as units of value in markets. Their role in trade was essential, as they facilitated exchanges between distant cities, even when the products exchanged were not directly valuable. For example, a Maya merchant might offer a certain quantity of shells in exchange for fine cloth or an obsidian tool, thus establishing a monetary system based on aesthetics and the availability of natural resources.

Archaeologists have discovered shells used as currency in the tombs of nobles and in important trading sites, such as the great markets of Tikal and Calakmul. These discoveries show that shells were not only a means of exchange, but also a status symbol. Elites accumulated shells to demonstrate their wealth, keeping them in caskets or displaying them at important ceremonies. The power of these objects went beyond their commercial utility, embodying prestige and influence.

The shellfish trade also illustrates the vast trade networks that the Maya had established throughout Mesoamerica. Spondylus shells, for example, came mainly from the waters of the Pacific, far from the jungles where the Maya lived. This means that these objects travelled great distances, passing from hand to hand through various exchanges, before arriving in the markets of Mayan cities. This network of trade, fuelled by the demand for these precious objects, demonstrates the interconnectedness of civilizations at the time and the importance of trade in Mayan economic development.

The symbolism of seashells as currency among the Maya reveals the extent to which their economy was rooted in the natural and cultural elements of their environment. Every shell, every transaction, carried with it a story of travel, value and prestige.

Fact 22 - Mayan houses withstood tropical conditions

The Maya lived in often harsh tropical environments, with heavy rainfall, strong winds and intense humidity. To adapt to these conditions, they built houses that were not only functional, but also perfectly suited to their climate. Traditional Mayan houses, called "na", were mainly made of local materials such as wood, thatch and clay. These materials were chosen not only for their availability, but also for their ability to withstand the elements and provide comfortable shelter.

The thatched roofs of Mayan houses were built at an angle to allow rainwater to run off quickly, thus preventing infiltration. This type of light, well-ventilated roof also provided good thermal insulation, keeping interiors cool on hot, humid days. Natural ventilation was a key element in the design of the houses, with doors and windows strategically placed to allow constant air circulation. This design reduced the heat inside, making the houses pleasant even in the hottest months.

House walls were often made of cob, a mixture of clay and plant fibers, applied to a wooden structure. This material had the advantage of being durable, while offering protection against insects and small creatures, common in tropical regions. In addition, cob acted as a moisture regulator, absorbing excess water during rains and releasing moisture during droughts, thus maintaining a stable and healthy indoor environment.

The Maya also built their houses on raised stone platforms, a technique that helped protect dwellings from the frequent flooding of tropical lowlands. These platforms provided a solid, durable base, preventing damage from flash floods. This elevation also improved ventilation under the floor, adding an extra layer of comfort and protection against ground humidity. These platforms also served to distinguish houses from muddy paths during the rainy season.

The design of Mayan houses reflected an intimate understanding of the environment and the needs of their inhabitants. They were not only refuges against the elements, but also harmonious living spaces that incorporated nature into their construction. Using local materials and intelligent construction techniques, the Maya built homes that withstood the test of time and climatic conditions.

Fact 23 - The Mayans followed the cycles of Venus

The Maya attached particular importance to Venus, whom they considered a powerful and influential star, often associated with the god Kukulcán. They followed its cycles with astonishing precision, integrating its movements into their calendars and rituals. Observations of Venus were an integral part of their astronomical system, and priest-astronomers meticulously noted its appearances at dawn and dusk. These 584-day cycles were used not only to predict celestial events, but also to guide political and military decisions.

The Maya had observed that Venus reappeared in the sky at regular intervals, a cycle they called the "sik'uh", or Venus cycle. These observations can be found in the Dresden Codex, one of the few surviving Mayan books. This codex contains detailed tables of Venus appearances, illustrating the depth and sophistication of their astronomical knowledge. The Maya knew how to predict the phases of Venus with such accuracy that they could foresee its appearances decades in advance, and these predictions played a crucial role in planning important events.

Venus was not only an astronomical curiosity for the Maya, it was also a symbol of power and war. Military leaders and kings consulted Venus' cycles to determine the best times to launch military expeditions or sign alliances. For example, Venus eclipses, when the planet temporarily disappeared from the sky, were seen as signs of bad luck or divine wrath. The Maya adapted their strategies and actions according to these observations, demonstrating the profound influence of Venus on their culture and politics.

Mayan observatories, such as the one at Chichen Itza, were specially oriented to track the movement of Venus and other celestial bodies. Priests would stand on these structures, carefully observing the rising and setting of Venus, recording every detail in their registers. These observations were then communicated to the rulers, who used them to adjust their ritual and agricultural calendars. The precision of these measurements shows just how connected the Maya were to cosmic cycles, using the heavens as a guide for daily life.

This relationship with Venus testifies to the ingenuity of the Maya and their ability to link astronomy to their culture and spirituality.

Fact 24 - Mayan languages were diverse and sophisticated

The Mayans spoke a variety of languages, forming a rich and complex linguistic group. Today, there are still over 30 different Mayan languages, all descended from an ancient common language called proto-maya, spoken over 4,000 years ago. These languages have diversified over time, with each city-state or region developing its own dialect or language. This diversity reflects the cultural complexity and political independence of the Mayan cities, each with its own unique linguistic identity.

Mayan languages weren't just used for everyday communication; they were also vectors of culture and sophisticated knowledge. They enabled scribes to write complex hieroglyphic texts, such as codexes and monument inscriptions, covering subjects as varied as astronomy, religious rituals, the history of royal dynasties, and cosmogonic myths. The Maya used systems of compound words and suffixes that added precise nuances to meanings, making their language suitable for expressing complex, abstract ideas.

The diversity of Mayan languages also influenced diplomacy and trade. Merchants and royal emissaries often had to be multilingual, able to navigate between different city-states with distinct languages. For example, a cocoa merchant from Tikal might encounter speakers of Yucatecan, Chol or Quiché on his trade journeys. This ability to communicate across different languages facilitated trade and alliances, while respecting the cultural particularities of each city.

Priests and nobles, often the only ones to have fully mastered writing, played a central role in preserving and transmitting these languages. They inscribed the exploits of kings and important events on stelae and monuments, using a language rich in symbolism and poetic expression. These inscriptions were intended not only to glorify the rulers, but also to serve as lasting witnesses for future generations, engraving history and culture in stone.

Today, Mayan languages continue to be spoken by millions of people in Central America, despite centuries of change and challenge. They are a living testimony to the heritage of the Maya and the resilience of their culture. Each Mayan language carries with it stories, traditions and ancient knowledge, reminding us of the richness of a civilization that was able to express its vision of the world with a depth and subtlety that few other cultures have matched.

Fact 25 - Mayan frescoes told colorful stories

The Maya excelled in the art of fresco, using the walls of their temples and palaces as canvases to tell vibrant, colorful stories. These frescoes were not merely decorative; they were visual narratives depicting scenes of daily life, religious rituals, epic battles and founding myths. Painted with natural pigments extracted from minerals and plants, frescoes were created with a palette of vivid colors that would stand the test of time, such as deep blues, bright reds and luminous greens.

A remarkable example can be found in the frescoes of Bonampak, an archaeological site in the jungles of Chiapas, Mexico. The walls of this ancient city are covered with paintings depicting war scenes, captives and elaborate ceremonies, offering a fascinating insight into Mayan society and its hierarchy. The frescoes show warriors in action, dressed in richly decorated costumes, and nobles participating in rituals, surrounded by musicians and dancers. These realistic, dynamic representations provide an insight into Mayan values and beliefs, showing the importance of war, victory and celebration in their culture.

Frescoes were also used to immortalize gods and myths. They often depicted major Mayan deities, such as Kukulcán and Chaac, engaged in acts of creation, destruction or blessing. In the San Bartolo frescoes, we can see the Mayan creation myth, with complex images depicting the Divine Corn and other cosmic figures in a harmonious dance that symbolizes the order of the universe. These paintings functioned as open books on the walls, explaining theological concepts to the faithful who contemplated them.

Frescoes were created by highly skilled artists, often commissioned by rulers or priests. These artists used elaborate techniques, such as "buon fresco", where pigments were applied to fresh plaster, allowing the colors to seep through and set durably. Frescoes were carefully planned, with every detail having a precise meaning, from the gestures of the figures to the patterns of the clothes and objects depicted. These works of art were not just decorations, but educational and spiritual tools, designed to teach and inspire.

The discovery and preservation of Mayan frescoes today offer a valuable insight into the complex and colorful world of this civilization.

Fact 26 - Mayan kings wore extravagant headdresses

Mayan kings were distinguished by their spectacular headdresses, which were not just fashion accessories, but true symbols of power and divinity. These often extremely elaborate headdresses were made from precious materials such as quetzal feathers, jade, gold and shells. Long, emerald-green quetzal feathers were particularly prized for their rarity and beauty. Wearing a headdress adorned with such feathers meant that the wearer was at the top of the social hierarchy and was perceived as an intermediary between gods and men.

Kings' headdresses were often so tall and imposing that they required the help of several assistants to put them on. They represented not only the wealth and status of the king, but also important symbolic motifs such as snakes, jaguars or divine figures. At Tikal, for example, sculptures show kings wearing headdresses in the shape of a jaguar's head, symbolizing strength and courage. These representations left no doubt as to the ruler's authority and connection to the powerful spirits of nature.

Ceremonies were key occasions when kings sported their most sumptuous headdresses. During rituals, sacrifices or festivals, kings would appear before the people adorned in their extravagant headdresses, accompanied by richly decorated garments and other royal regalia. Headdresses served to amplify the king's stature, making him appear taller and more imposing, reinforcing his image as a powerful, almost divine ruler. Each headdress was unique, designed to reflect the king's specific qualities, lineage and achievements.

Frescoes and stelae found at archaeological sites such as Palenque and Copán show meticulous details of these headdresses, illustrating the care and craftsmanship required to create them. Maya craftsmen must have had great expertise in working with such diverse materials, combining feathers, precious stones and metals in aesthetic harmony. These headdresses were not only fashion masterpieces, but also true proclamations of Mayan skill and creativity.

The headdresses of Mayan kings remain among the most emblematic symbols of this civilization. They embody the cultural richness of the Maya and their ability to express power through art and ritual. Each headdress, with its complexity and brilliance, told the story of a king, his reign and his place in the cosmic order. By wearing them, kings affirmed their role as earthly and celestial leaders, uniting the visible and invisible through these extraordinary adornments.

Fact 27 - The Mayans used calendars to predict the seasons

The Maya had remarkably accurate calendars that enabled them to predict the seasons and structure their daily life, rituals and agricultural activities. The Mayan solar calendar, known as the Haab, consisted of 365 days, divided into 18 months of 20 days each, plus an additional 5-day period called the Wayeb, considered a period of bad luck. This calendar was used to synchronize harvests with the seasons, marking key moments such as the planting and harvesting of maize, the Maya staple food.

The Maya didn't just follow a single calendar; they used several in parallel for specific purposes. The Tzolk'in, a 260-day ritual calendar, was used to plan religious events and important ceremonies. By combining the Haab and the Tzolk'in, they created a longer cycle called the 52-year Round, which symbolized the convergence of these calendars and represented a cycle of renewal in their cosmology. This complex combination enabled events to be predicted with great accuracy, ensuring that human activities remained in harmony with natural and cosmic cycles.

Mayan calendars were based on meticulous observations of the movements of the Sun, Moon and stars. Astronomical priests used specific landmarks in temples and observatories to mark the solstices and equinoxes, which indicated seasonal changes. These architectural alignments defined precise times for agricultural rituals, guaranteeing abundant harvests and protecting the community against periods of drought or flood. This mastery of natural cycles gave the Maya an essential advantage in managing their resources.

Inscriptions found on stelae and monuments show that the Maya used these calendars not only for agriculture, but also to mark important historical events, such as the births and coronations of kings, military victories, and even important celestial alignments. Dates inscribed in hieroglyphs on monuments testify to their sophisticated use of calendars to structure time and history. Priests and scribes kept precise records that were consulted when making crucial decisions, demonstrating the importance of calendars in the management of social and political life.

By linking the cycle of the seasons to human activities, Mayan calendars reflected a vision of the world in which each moment resonated with the rhythms of nature.

Fact 28 - Mayan hanging gardens fed their cities

The Maya were masters in the art of agriculture, and to feed their great cities, they set up ingenious hanging gardens called "chinampas". These gardens, often built on artificial islands in the middle of swamps and lakes, optimized the use of space while providing fertile soil for growing essential crops such as corn, beans, squash and other medicinal plants. Chinampas were created by piling up layers of mud, decomposed vegetation and other organic materials, producing rich, well-watered soil.

These hanging gardens were surrounded by canals, which facilitated natural irrigation and maintained a constant level of humidity, essential for crops in the tropical and sometimes arid climates of the Mayan regions. The Maya knew that the water from the canals brought nutrients to the soil, making the chinampas extremely productive and capable of supporting large populations. As well as providing food, these gardens also contributed to the local ecosystem, attracting birds, fish and other animals that were part of Mayan diets and rituals.

Chinampas were not only agricultural solutions, but also examples of harmony between man and nature, a central principle in Mayan culture. By making sustainable use of available natural resources, the Maya were able to cultivate land otherwise unsuitable for farming. Cities such as Tenochtitlan and Tikal, for example, although located in difficult environments, were able to prosper thanks to these innovations. Hanging gardens enabled crops to be produced all year round, regardless of the season, reducing the risk of famine and ensuring a continuous supply of food for the inhabitants.

The techniques used to build and maintain the hanging gardens required precise know-how and rigorous organization. Farmers had to regularly maintain the chinampas by cleaning the canals and adding new organic materials to maintain soil fertility. These tasks were often performed in community, reflecting the importance of cooperation for the well-being of the city. Hanging gardens were not only places of food production, but also symbols of Mayan resilience and ingenuity in the face of environmental challenges.

The remains of hanging gardens, still visible today in certain regions, bear witness to the efficiency and importance of these structures in Mayan society. They show how the Maya knew how to make the most of their environment, transforming inhospitable terrain into veritable oases of food production.

Fact 29 - The Maya built observation platforms

The Maya were keen observers of the heavens, and to refine their astronomical knowledge, they built observation platforms dedicated to studying the movements of the Sun, Moon, stars and planets. These platforms, often located atop pyramids or on isolated structures, offered an unobstructed view of the horizon, enabling priest astronomers to follow the celestial cycles with precision. At Uxmal, for example, the "El Adivino" observatory is an elevated structure that allowed observation of the solstices and equinoxes, crucial times for planning rituals and agricultural work.

These observation platforms were not simply viewpoints; they were designed with specific alignments to capture important astronomical phenomena. Mayan architects used markers and precise orientations to indicate the positions of the sun at sunrise and sunset on key dates of the year. At Chichen Itza, the temple of Kukulcán is famous for its alignments marking the spring equinox, creating the illusion of a snake descending the stairs, symbolizing Kukulcán itself. These alignments were not just architectural feats, but tools for measuring and understanding time.

Observation platforms also played a central role in weather prediction and the management of agricultural seasons. By tracking the movement of the stars and planets, the Maya could anticipate rainy and dry seasons, adjusting their agricultural calendars to maximize harvests. Observatories, such as those found at Copán, served as centers of learning where priests trained in astronomy studied and recorded their observations, contributing to the elaborate calendars that guided Mayan life.

Inscriptions and sculptures found on the viewing platforms reveal that these places were also sites of power and prestige. Kings and priests used these platforms to assert their connection with the divine, claiming to receive messages from the gods through the stars. These platforms became symbols of knowledge and authority, and the ceremonies held there reinforced the idea that rulers possessed a sacred understanding of the world's cycles. Depictions of kings observing the heavens testify to the political and spiritual importance of these structures.

Mayan observation platforms show just how fascinated this civilization was by the cosmos, and how determined they were to understand the natural laws that governed their existence.

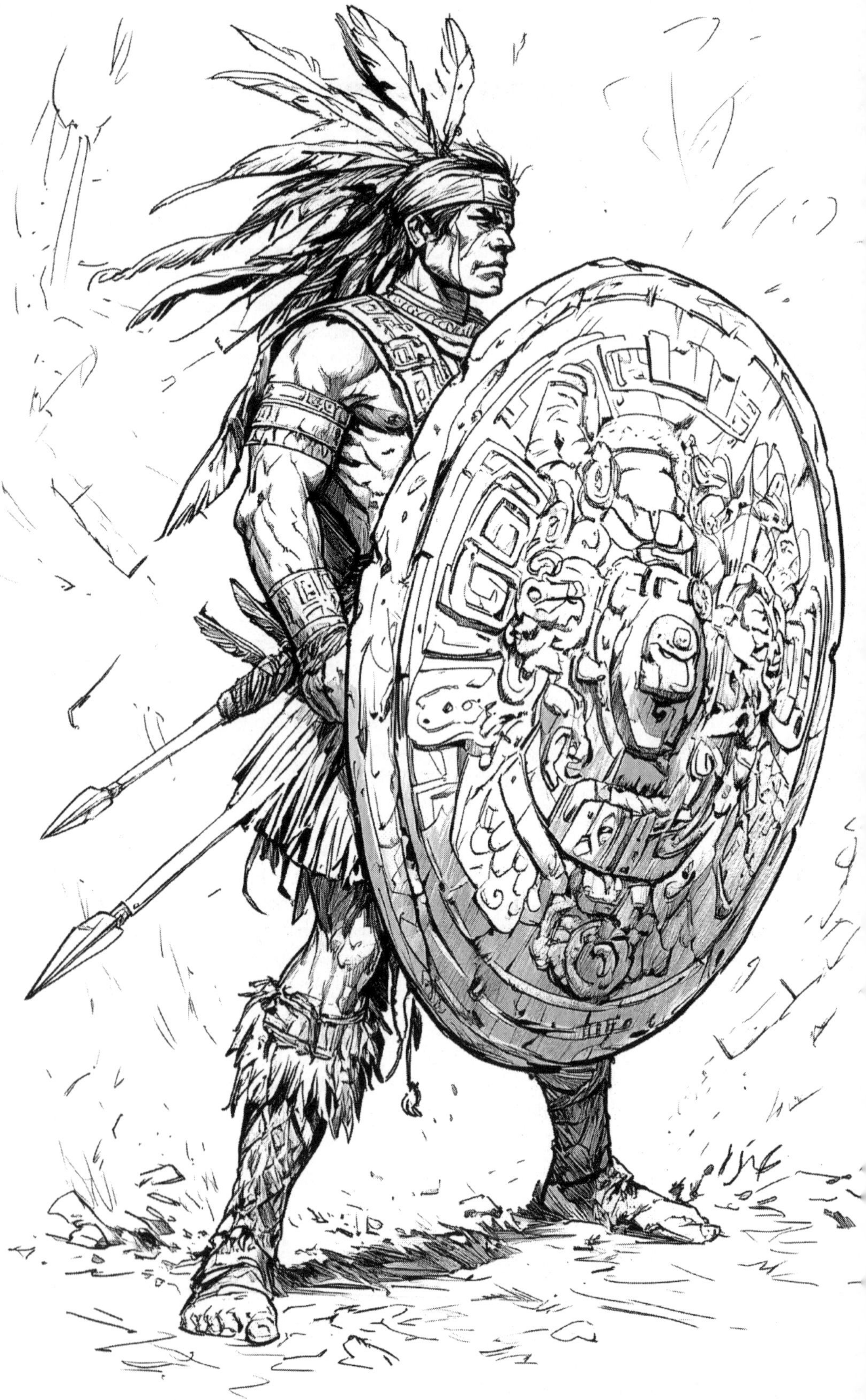

Fact 30 - Mayan warriors used wooden shields

Mayan warriors protected themselves on the battlefield with wooden shields, skilfully crafted to combine lightness and strength. These shields, often decorated with colorful motifs and tribal symbols, reflected the rank and courage of the wearer. Made from local woods such as ceiba, they were strong enough to deflect spears, arrows and projectiles thrown by the enemy. Some shields were reinforced with layers of leather or braided fiber strips, increasing durability without compromising maneuverability.

Shields were often adorned with feathers, jade or paintings depicting powerful animals such as jaguars or eagles, symbolizing strength and agility. Elite warriors, known as "jaguar warriors" or "eagle warriors", wore particularly elaborate shields, indicating their superior status on the battlefield. These ornaments not only served to intimidate the enemy, but also served as a reminder of the protection of the gods and the honor of fighting for their city. Each shield was unique, reflecting the personality and exploits of its owner.

In addition to their defensive function, shields also served as symbols of identity and communication. The motifs painted on shields could represent alliances, past victories or affiliations with specific groups. For example, designs of snakes could signal a connection with the god Kukulcán, while symbols of rain and lightning could invoke the blessing of the rain god, Chaac. These representations were intended to inspire awe and respect, while boosting troop morale.

Wooden shields were often used in combination with other Mayan weapons, such as spears, short swords called "macuahuitl" and slings. Warriors knew how to use these shields dynamically, moving quickly around the battlefield to parry attacks and strike back effectively. Shields enabled warriors to get closer to the enemy while minimizing the risk of serious injury. The mobility and flexibility offered by wooden shields were crucial in close combat, where every move could make the difference between victory and defeat.

Mayan warriors' shields illustrate their ingenuity and profound understanding of warfare. They were not merely utilitarian objects, but extensions of Mayan culture, integrating art, spirituality and military strategy. Wearing these shields, warriors embodied the spirit of their people, ready to defend their land and their gods with bravery and honor.

Fact 31 - The stelae recounted the exploits of kings

Mayan stelae, large upright stones engraved with hieroglyphs and sculpted figures, played an essential role in transmitting the history and exploits of kings. Erected in the central squares of city-states, they were used as commemorative monuments to glorify sovereigns and recall their military victories, diplomatic alliances and religious achievements. Each stele was a testament to the king's power and tangible proof of his ability to maintain order and prosperity in his city.

Inscriptions on stelae were often written in rich, poetic language, intended to impress and inspire those who read them. They not only recounted the Facts, but also magnified the kings, comparing them to gods or emphasizing their role as mediators between the terrestrial and celestial worlds. For example, on the Copán stelae, King 18-Rabbit is depicted wearing divine symbols, surrounded by images of gods and warriors, reinforcing his status as a god-king.

Steles were also used to mark specific events in time, such as coronations, temple dedications or eclipses, which the Maya considered to be important signs. Thanks to their complex dating system, the Maya were able to inscribe exact dates on stelae, providing a permanent calendar of major events. These stone chronicles were invaluable not only to the Maya themselves, but also to modern archaeologists, who can trace the history of Maya cities through the engraved narratives.

The creation of a stele was an event in itself, requiring the work of numerous craftsmen, sculptors and scribes. Every detail, from the engraving of the hieroglyphs to the sculpted figures, was executed with remarkable precision. The steles were often decorated with bas-reliefs showing the kings in triumphant poses, dressed in their finest finery, with extravagant headdresses and symbolic scepters. These sculptures depicted the kings in all their splendor, conveying their authority and connection with the divine to all who passed by.

The steles, with their imposing presence and detailed accounts, served as reference points for future generations, constantly recalling the greatness of the kings and the events that had shaped the city. They were more than mere monuments; they were books in stone, perennial accounts of a glorious history. Each stele recounted a part of the city's life, bringing to life the triumphs and challenges the kings had faced.

Fact 32 - Obsidian jewelry was prized by the Mayans

Obsidian, a deep, shiny black volcanic rock, held a special place in Mayan culture, not only as a material for tools and weapons, but also for elegant and prized jewelry. The Maya used this stone to create delicate ornaments such as necklaces, pendants, bracelets and earrings. Obsidian jewelry was particularly prized for its mysterious brilliance and its ability to be polished to reflect light, giving these pieces an almost magical allure.

Obsidian was also associated with spiritual and symbolic properties, reinforcing its value. The Maya believed that obsidian had the power to ward off evil spirits and protect the wearer. Obsidian jewelry was not just a beauty accessory, but a protective talisman, often worn during rituals and important ceremonies. Priests and nobles wore obsidian jewelry to distinguish themselves and assert their high status in society, as obsidian was also a symbol of power and authority.

The manufacture of obsidian jewelry required great skill. Mayan craftsmen worked this hard stone using precise cutting and polishing techniques, transforming rough blocks into finely detailed pieces. The process was laborious and required an in-depth knowledge of obsidian's properties, notably its fragility, which could render the stone brittle if not handled correctly. The resulting jewels, often adorned with geometric motifs or animal figures, reflected the expertise and talent of the craftsmen, who knew how to bring out the natural beauty of the stone.

The importance of obsidian in the Maya world is also demonstrated by its trade. Obsidian deposits were found mainly in remote mountain regions, and the stone had to be transported over long distances to cities such as Tikal or Palenque. This trade attested to the value of obsidian, as it was not only sought after for jewelry, but also as a currency in the complex trade networks of Mesoamerica. Obsidian objects, including jewelry, circulated between cities, strengthening economic and cultural ties between the Maya and their neighbors.

Obsidian jewelry remains a fascinating testimony to Mayan ingenuity and culture. These pieces, with their dark lustre and elegant shapes, are a reminder of how the Maya knew how to transform natural resources into objects of great aesthetic and spiritual value.

Fact 33 - The Maya celebrated the cycles of the sun

The Maya attached sacred importance to the cycles of the sun, which they saw as the beating heart of the universe, regulating the passage of time and the rhythms of daily life. They closely followed the sun's movements and celebrated solstices and equinoxes with elaborate ceremonies to honor solar deities. These celebrations marked key moments in their agricultural calendar, indicating propitious times for sowing, harvesting or performing sacred rituals. The sun, symbolizing life and fertility, was central to their cosmology and culture.

Mayan sites were often built according to solar alignments, to amplify the link between human structures and cosmic cycles. At Chichen Itza, the Kukulcán temple is famous for the illusion of the serpent descending its steps during the equinoxes, a phenomenon made possible by the interplay of sunlight and shadow. This impressive display of symbolic architecture shows how the Maya used their knowledge of the sun to create powerful spiritual and visual experiences. Solstices and equinoxes were seen as moments when the gates of heaven opened, enabling a direct connection with the gods.

As astronomers and guardians of the calendar, Mayan priests played a central role in solar celebrations. They made precise observations from observation platforms, noting the positions of the sun to predict seasonal changes and plan rituals accordingly. On major solar festivals, such as those at the winter solstice, offerings were made to thank the sun for its return and implore its blessing on future harvests. These rituals included song, dance and sometimes sacrifice, all aimed at maintaining the balance between man and cosmic forces.

The cycles of the sun were also integrated into Mayan daily life, influencing not only their agricultural practices, but also their beliefs about life after death and rebirth. They saw the sun's daily journey across the sky as a metaphor for the cycle of life: birth, death and rebirth. This understanding was reflected in their funeral rituals, where the orientation of tombs and offerings was aimed at aligning the deceased with the solar cycles, ensuring a harmonious passage to the afterlife.

Mayan solar celebrations show just how connected this civilization was to the universe around them. By honoring the sun, they recognized its power as the source of all life and its role as a guide in their earthly existence.

Fact 34 - The Maya built sturdy suspension bridges

The Maya, renowned for their architectural ingenuity, also built suspension bridges to link different parts of their cities, crossing rivers, ravines and swamps. These bridges were essential structures that facilitated trade, military travel and daily life, enabling inhabitants to cross difficult terrain with ease. Maya suspension bridges were mainly built using natural materials such as lianas, wood and woven plant fibers, which offered both flexibility and strength.

The design of these bridges was ingenious. The Maya would stretch strong vines across a ravine or river, then attach them to stone or wooden pillars, stabilizing the structure. Wooden planks were then laid over these cables to form the bridge surface. This construction method enabled bridges to adapt to movements and vibrations, making crossing safe even in strong winds or changing water flows. Bridges could be of various sizes, some being long enough to link important portions of their extensive road networks.

Suspension bridges also played an important strategic role in the defense of cities. In the event of conflict, the Maya could cut or destroy these bridges to prevent the advance of enemies, using their knowledge of the terrain to their advantage. These structures were not only tools of mobility, but also tactical elements in the protection of their territory. Bridges enabled the control of communication and trade routes, which was crucial to the management of the economy and security of Mayan city-states.

Accounts and drawings by Spanish explorers, long after the classical Maya period, describe with wonder the solidity and functionality of these suspension bridges. Some bridges were so well built that they remained in use long after the fall of the main Mayan cities, testifying to the durability and quality of their design. Suspension bridges demonstrate how the Maya knew how to exploit the natural resources of their environment to meet their practical needs, while at the same time demonstrating their ability to meet complex architectural challenges.

Today, although most Mayan suspension bridges have disappeared due to erosion and the passage of time, their existence continues to impress by the ingenuity and technical mastery they represented. The remains of these structures, along with illustrations and historical descriptions, serve as a reminder of the Maya's ability to build infrastructures adapted to their environment.

Fact 35 - The Maya carved monumental statues

The Maya were true masters in the art of monumental sculpture, creating impressive statues to adorn their cities and reflect their vision of the world. These sculptures, often carved from local limestone, represented gods, kings and mythological figures, embodying both the spiritual and political power of the Maya civilization. The statues could reach several meters in height and were richly detailed, with intricate patterns carved into clothing, headdresses and accessories, illustrating the wealth and importance of the figures depicted.

One of the most emblematic statues is that of King Pakal of Palenque, depicted on his sarcophagus with a majestic posture, wearing an elaborate headdress and sumptuous jewels. Carved with incredible precision, this statue shows Pakal being reborn in the afterlife, surrounded by cosmic symbols. Mayan sculptors used stone and wood tools to work the hard stone, making their level of detail and finesse of execution all the more impressive. These statues were not simply decorations; they were vehicles for divine messages and mythological narratives.

Monumental statues were often placed in strategic locations, such as central squares, temples or entrances to royal complexes, where they could be seen by the greatest number of people. They served as focal points during public ceremonies, drawing spectators' attention to the stories engraved in stone. At Copán, for example, statues of kings lined up along the hieroglyphic staircase recount the conquests and exploits of the sovereigns, celebrating their victories and their divine right to rule. These sculptures were propaganda tools, designed to inspire respect and loyalty in their subjects.

In addition to carving human figures, the Maya also depicted sacred animals such as jaguars, snakes and birds, symbolizing various natural and divine forces. These animal representations were often stylized and integrated into complex geometric patterns, reflecting the harmony between the natural and spiritual worlds. Sculptors played with proportions, textures and shapes to bring these figures to life, creating works of art that were both realistic and imbued with symbolism.

Monumental Mayan statues continue to fascinate with their size, detail and meaning. They bear witness to the artistic skill of the sculptors and to the Maya's deep connection with their spiritual and social environment.

Fact 36 - The Mayans invented games with dice

The Maya were not only remarkable builders and astronomers, they also had a keen sense of play and entertainment, which they integrated into their daily lives. Among the games they played, some used dice, demonstrating their taste for strategic challenges and chance. Maya dice, often carved in bone, wood or stone, were engraved with symbols or numbers that enabled them to play various board games, the rules of which, although partially lost, emphasized luck and skill.

These dice games were not only a form of entertainment, but also a means of teaching and practicing skills such as strategy, quick decision-making and risk management. Archaeologists have discovered dice in contexts that suggest these games may also have had ritual or divinatory connotations, with the results of throws sometimes interpreted as messages from the gods. Games with dice were thus deeply integrated into Mayan culture, going beyond the simple pastime to touch on spiritual aspects of life.

The dice themselves were often elaborately decorated, the engraved symbols being not only functional but also aesthetically pleasing. The geometric figures and patterns engraved on the dice were often linked to Mayan cosmology, including symbols of days, months or even natural elements such as the sun and rain. The Maya believed that these elements brought a sacred aspect to the game, reinforcing the link between the player, the natural world and the spirit world. Dice thus became precious objects, carefully crafted and sometimes handed down from generation to generation.

Dice games were played by nobles and commoners alike, although the more elaborate, ritualized versions were probably reserved for the elite. At festivities or public gatherings, it was not uncommon to see groups of people gathered around a game board, the spirit of competition and the pleasure of the game transcending social barriers. Games created a space where individual skills could be tested, but also where social bonds were strengthened, underlining the importance of community in Mayan society.

Today, the dice found on archaeological digs continue to captivate with their simplicity and complexity. They remind us that, despite technological advances and great works of architecture, the Maya were also a people who enjoyed moments of leisure and competition.

Fact 37 - Natural pigments colored Mayan frescoes

The Maya used natural pigments to bring their frescoes to life, transforming the walls of their temples and palaces into veritable colorful narratives. These pigments, extracted from minerals, plants and even insects, were used to create a palette of vibrant colors, from brilliant blues to deep reds and intense greens. The famous Mayan blue, for example, was made from a combination of indigo, extracted from a plant, and palygorskite clay, a complex recipe that testified to the skill of Mayan artists.

Frescoes were often painted over a layer of fresh plaster, a technique known as "buon fresco", which allowed the pigments to seep into the wall surface and set durably. This process ensured not only the vividness of the colors, but also their resistance to time. Frescoes like those discovered at Bonampak, with their dynamic scenes of battle, ritual and daily life, show just how essential these colors were for conveying stories and emotions. These frescoes were not only works of art, but also visual documents that captivated viewers with their brilliance.

Mayan artists mastered the use of pigments to create contrasts and subtle details, bringing figures and scenes on frescoes almost to life. Red, often obtained from hematite, was used to represent skin, royal garments and symbols of power. Greens and blues, associated with vegetation and deities, were applied with precision to reinforce the importance of certain characters or fresco elements. Yellows, derived from ochre, added a touch of light and warmth, balancing the complex compositions of these murals.

The application of pigments was not only a question of aesthetics, but also of symbolic meaning. Each color had a particular value in Mayan cosmology: red symbolized the sun and life, blue was linked to sacrifice and purification rituals, while green represented nature and fertility. Colored frescoes were therefore powerful means of communication, linking art to the spirituality and deep-rooted beliefs of the Maya. They were often located in sacred spaces, where bright colors amplified the mystical atmosphere of the place.

The natural pigments in Mayan frescoes are a testament to their ability to draw on their environment to create lasting and meaningful artistic expressions. Despite the centuries, these colors continue to shine in the ruins of Mayan cities, reminding us of the visual and symbolic richness of this civilization.

Fact 38 - The Mayans believed in a multi-storey world

The Maya saw the world as a complex structure divided into several levels, each with its own meaning and inhabitants. Their cosmological vision included three main levels: the underworld, the land of the living and the sky. Each of these levels was itself divided into sub-levels, creating a hierarchy of existence in which gods, spirits and humans constantly interacted. This structured model profoundly influenced their religion, architecture and daily rituals.

The underworld, known as Xibalba, was a place of mystery and challenge, often described as a dark realm inhabited by fearsome gods and spirits. Unlike other cultures, which saw the underworld as purely negative, the Maya saw Xibalba as a necessary passageway for transformation and renewal. The dead passed through this world to reach the afterlife, and mythological heroes, such as the twins Hunahpu and Xbalanque, undertook trials there to challenge the lords of Xibalba, as recounted in the Popol Vuh, a sacred Mayan text.

Above Xibalba was the land of the living, the level where humans lived and interacted with nature and the gods. The Maya believed that their terrestrial world was at the center of the universe, supported by the branches of a great sacred tree called the Ceiba, which linked the underworld to the heavens. This concept of a cosmic axis was represented in their temples and pyramids, often designed to symbolize this connection between the three levels of the cosmos. The rituals, offerings and sacrifices performed by the Maya aimed to maintain balance and harmony between these worlds.

Heaven, the upper level, was divided into thirteen tiers, each governed by different deities associated with the natural elements, celestial bodies and the forces of fate. The Maya believed that the virtuous souls of the deceased could access these celestial heights, where they would find eternal peace. Observation temples and pyramids, often aligned with the movements of the sun and stars, reflected this quest for spiritual elevation. Representations of the sky in Mayan art included symbols of snakes, birds and stars, reminding us of the importance of celestial observation in understanding the divine will.

This layered conception of the world was not limited to a simple religious belief; it structured the entire Maya worldview, influencing the way they built their cities, celebrated their rites and understood their place in the universe.

Fact 39 - The Maya used earthbows for their ceremonies

The Maya built earthen arches, also known as "arcos falsos", to mark ritual passages and sacred spaces in their ceremonies. These structures, often made of earth, stone and vegetation, served to symbolize the link between the world of men and the world of the gods. Earthen arches were commonly used for ceremonies of passage, such as rites of passage to adulthood, weddings or fertility rituals. By passing under these bows, participants were considered to be entering a sacred space, under the protection of Mayan deities.

These arches were not just architectural elements, but powerful symbols of transformation and rebirth. They were decorated with leaves, flowers and sometimes ritual paintings, representing natural and divine elements. For example, the snake and bird motifs added to the bows represented protective spirits and spirit guides, ensuring the gods' blessing on participants. These bows also represented the gates of the cosmos, opening a symbolic path between the different levels of the Mayan world, from the celestial underground to the heavens.

Earthen arches also had a practical function in ceremonies, serving as focal points for offerings and prayers. The Maya often placed sacred objects, such as censers, figurines or food, around and under these arches to honor the gods and ask for their favor. The smoke from the incense, rising through the arch, symbolized the ascent of prayers to the heavens. The earthen arches were places where the community could gather to express its devotion and renew its ties with the divine forces.

These structures were generally ephemeral, built specifically for particular ceremonies and often dismantled or left to decompose naturally after the event. This reflected the Mayan vision of the world as being in constant transformation, where even the most sacred structures had to return to the earth. Earthbows, though temporary, left a lasting impression on participants and on the community's collective memory, reminding us of the power of ritual and the importance of passage between worlds.

The use of earthen arches demonstrates the ingenuity of the Maya in integrating nature and architecture into their spiritual practices. These arches, simple in construction but rich in symbolism, show how the Maya used elements of their environment to create spaces for spiritual transformation and connection with the divine.

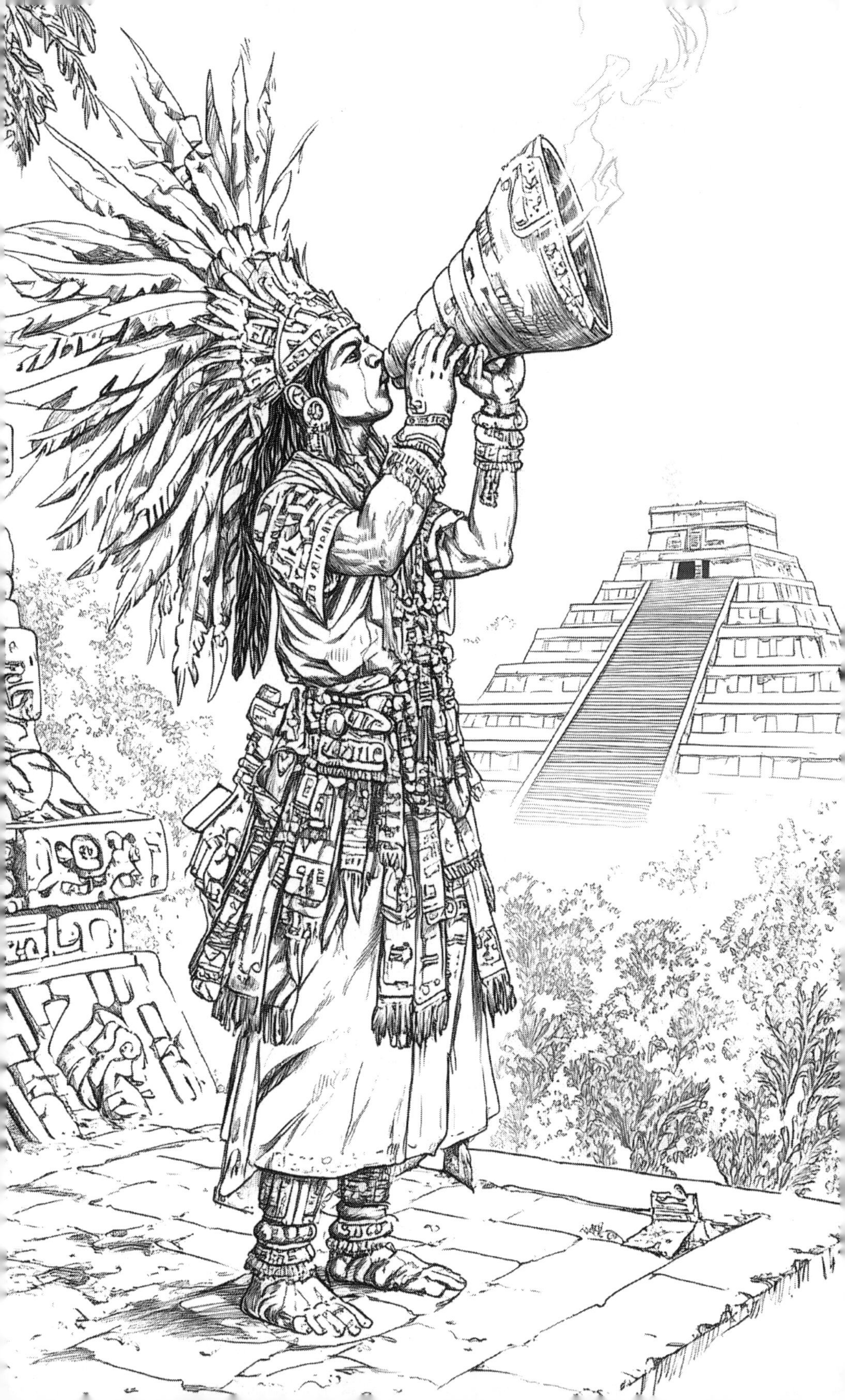

Fact 40 - The Maya used conches as instruments

The Maya were experts at using marine conch shells as musical instruments, transforming them into powerful tools of communication and ritual. The conches, carefully pierced at a precise point, served as natural trumpets whose deep, resonant sound could be heard from great distances. They were often used in religious ceremonies, processions and even on battlefields, where their sound was used to galvanize troops or send signals to warriors.

The use of conches went far beyond music; they were powerful symbols of the sea, fertility and the gods. The sounds produced by these instruments were perceived as echoes of the voices of deities, particularly those associated with water and rain, such as Chaac, the rain god. In rituals, the sound of conches could symbolize a call to the gods to ask for their blessing or intervention. Through these instruments, priests and shamans communicated with the spirits, reinforcing the importance of conches in religious practices.

Conches were also decorated with engraved motifs, often depicting mythological scenes, sacred animals or astrological symbols. These decorations added a visual dimension to the conches, transforming them into objects of art and devotion. The Maya knew that each conch had a unique voice, depending on its size, shape and location. This diversity created a range of sounds that could be used in a variety of ways during ceremonies, from distant calls to soothing, gentle melodies.

In addition to their ritual use, conches had a practical function in everyday Maya life. They were used to mark the start of important meetings, to announce events or alerts, and even to bring communities together for public announcements. Conches thus played a key role in communication, particularly in large cities where their sound carried easily through squares and streets. They were versatile instruments, capable of transcending the simple limits of music to become tools of social and spiritual cohesion.

The Maya's use of conches demonstrates their ability to integrate natural elements into their culture in creative and meaningful ways. These instruments didn't just produce sound; they carried with them stories, beliefs and sacred powers. Maya conches, with their unique sound and rich symbolism, remain a fascinating testament to the way the Maya used the resources of their environment to enrich their spiritual and daily lives.

Fact 41 - The Maya used steam baths to purify their bodies

The Maya used to practice steam baths, called "temazcal", in specially built structures for the purification of body and mind. These steam baths were considered sacred rituals, designed not only to cleanse the body of physical impurities, but also to purify the soul and draw closer to the gods. Made of stone and earth, temazcals were small, dark, heated chambers, often dome-shaped, where water was poured over hot stones to create steam.

These steam baths were of great importance in the daily and spiritual life of the Maya. They were used before important rituals, such as wedding ceremonies or sacrifices, to purify and prepare spiritually. Warriors took steam baths before battles to fortify themselves, and after battles to eliminate the "toxins" of war. The temazcal was also a place of healing, where the sick came to be cured through heat and steam, sometimes combined with medicinal herbs and prayers.

The steam bath experience was seen as a rebirth. On entering the temazcal, participants were compared to children returning to the womb of the Earth. The heat and steam recreated a symbolic environment of creation and transformation. The Maya believed that this environment reproduced the conditions of the world's genesis, offering an opportunity for physical and spiritual renewal. Priests and shamans often supervised these rituals, guiding participants through chants and invocations to reinforce the bath's purifying effect.

Temazcals were not only reserved for collective rituals. They were also part of personal hygiene practices for many Mayan families, who regularly used them as domestic baths. The construction of temazcals was simple but effective: a small entrance allowed the heat inside to be controlled, and the design of the dome favoured the circulation of steam. Using the natural resources at their disposal, the Mayans had devised a steam bath system that was both practical and deeply rooted in their spiritual beliefs.

Today, the remains of these temazcals and the descriptions left in chronicles show us just how integral the practice of steam bathing was to Mayan culture. They reflect a sophisticated understanding of the benefits of heat and steam for the human body, but also a keen sense of the need for spiritual purification.

Fact 42 - The Maya built drainage systems

The Maya, masters of urban engineering, developed sophisticated drainage systems to manage rainwater in their cities, which were often exposed to extreme climatic conditions. These systems were essential to prevent flooding and protect urban structures from water damage. By using canals, conduits and retention wells, they were able to effectively control the flow of water, guaranteeing the durability of their buildings and public spaces. These works testify to their advanced understanding of hydraulics and the importance they attached to urban planning.

In large cities like Tikal, drainage systems were particularly elaborate. Channels cut in stone guided water from the roofs of buildings to underground reservoirs, where it could be stored for periods of drought. The Maya also used filters made of sand and stone to purify the water before it reached these reservoirs, showing remarkable attention to the quality of the water consumed. This attention to detail in water management demonstrates the extent to which the Maya understood the importance of this vital resource to the survival of their cities.

Drainage systems were not only functional, but also harmoniously integrated into the urban landscape. Canals were often covered with stone slabs, allowing residents to walk freely over them without being hindered by water run-off. Some of these canals also served as decorative walkways, lined with sculptures and plants, transforming a simple infrastructure into an aesthetic element that enriched the urban environment. In Palenque, for example, archaeologists have discovered beautifully decorated canals that prove that for the Maya, functionality and beauty went hand in hand.

The ingenuity of Mayan drainage systems also extended to agriculture, where canals were used to irrigate fields and control water levels in swampy areas. These systems maximized the use of farmland, even in difficult conditions, by ensuring that soils were neither too dry nor too flooded. This illustrates the Maya's ability to adapt their environment to meet their food needs while maintaining an ecological balance. Their expertise in water management contributed directly to the prosperity of their cities.

The remains of these drainage systems, still visible today in the ruins of many Mayan cities, are a reminder of the importance this civilization placed on the planning and sustainable management of resources.

Fact 43 - Ceramic masks were used for ritual purposes

The Maya made ceramic masks for use in their rituals, symbolizing divine forces, ancestors or mythological figures. These masks were not mere accessories; they had a profound meaning and served as a link between the world of humans and that of the gods. The masks, often finely sculpted and painted, represented human faces, animals or fantastical creatures, each with a specific function in the ceremonies. Wearing a mask during a ritual meant taking on the role of a deity or spirit, enabling participants to transform themselves and connect with supernatural powers.

Ceramic masks were particularly used for ceremonies of passage, such as initiations or funeral rites. At noble funerals, for example, masks representing gods of the afterlife were often placed over the faces of the deceased to protect and guide them on their journey to the next world. These masks, decorated with intricate designs and precious stones such as jade or obsidian, testified to the social status and spiritual role of the person buried. They were not simply decorative objects, but essential elements of transitional rituals.

Ceramic masks were also used for seasonal celebrations and religious festivities. Priests and dancers wearing these masks performed ritual dances, imitating the movements of gods or sacred animals to invoke their presence and blessings. For example, during rituals to call down rain, dancers wearing frog or snake masks, symbols of water and fertility, would mimic the rain dance. Masks served as a bridge between the material and spiritual worlds, making visible the invisible powers that ruled nature.

Ceramic masks were not only used for their spiritual significance, but also to tell stories and pass on teachings. In some ceremonies, masks represented characters from legends and myths, playing key roles in stories that taught participants life lessons, moral values or historical knowledge. Masks could represent legendary heroes, kings or warriors, and by wearing them, the actors became spokespersons for the collective story, reminding everyone of the lessons of the past and their duties to the community.

Fact 44 - Caves were sacred places for the Mayans

For the Maya, caves were much more than mere geological formations; they were seen as portals to the underworld, Xibalba, and played a central role in their spirituality. Caves were regarded as places of power where gods and spirits resided. By entering a cave, the Maya believed they were entering the domain of the deities, a sacred space conducive to rituals and offerings. These underground spaces were therefore used for important ceremonies, such as fertility rituals, rain offerings and purification rites.

One of the most famous caves in Mayan culture is the Loltún cave, located on the Yucatán peninsula. Used for thousands of years as a ceremonial site, the Maya left offerings such as pottery, obsidian tools and even the remains of sacrificial animals. These objects, found by archaeologists, testify to the importance of this site to the ancient Maya. The walls of some of these caves are adorned with paintings and engravings depicting deities, animals and cosmic symbols, further underlining their role as portals between worlds.

Rituals in the caves often included offerings of copal, a sacred resin burnt for its fragrant fumes, which were believed to nourish the gods and carry human prayers to the divine world. Priests and shamans conducted ceremonies in these damp, dark environments, where the flickering light of torches created a mystical atmosphere. The caves, with their stalactite and stalagmite formations, were also seen as physical manifestations of divine energy, making each ceremony even more solemn and charged with meaning.

Caves also had a practical function as water sources in certain regions where surface rivers were scarce. Cenotes, natural wells connected to underground cave systems, were particularly sacred. The Maya believed that these bodies of water were direct gateways to Xibalba, and that they were home to powerful spirits. Ceremonies around the cenotes often included sacrifices, ranging from small offerings of precious objects to, in extreme cases, human sacrifice, in the hope of appeasing the deities and guaranteeing abundant rainfall.

Today, the exploration of these caves by archaeologists continues to reveal the extent of their importance in Mayan culture.

Fact 45 - The Maya developed advanced irrigation techniques

Faced with a variety of environments, from dense jungles to arid regions, the Mayans developed sophisticated irrigation techniques to maximize their agricultural production. They devised ingenious systems to capture, store and distribute water, ensuring the survival of their crops even in times of drought. For example, in the Yucatán plains, where surface rivers are rare, they built reservoirs and canals to collect rainwater, called aguadas, which were used to irrigate fields throughout the year.

One of the most impressive techniques used by the Maya was that of chinampas, floating gardens created on lakes or swamps. By building platforms of enriched earth on foundations of reeds and branches, the Maya transformed marshy areas into fertile farmland. These gardens were naturally irrigated by the surrounding water, which not only increased crop yields but also reduced the need for manual watering. Chinampas were particularly effective for growing corn, beans and squash, the staples of the Mayan diet.

In mountainous regions, the Maya built terraces to cultivate steep slopes. These terraces, supported by stone walls, prevented soil erosion and helped retain rainwater. Canals and gullies dug between the terraces allowed water to be directed in a controlled manner, ensuring regular and efficient irrigation. This terraced cultivation method demonstrated intelligent adaptation to the difficult terrain and helped stabilize the soil while increasing the area available for cultivation.

The Maya also used complex canal systems to divert water from rivers to their fields. At Tikal, canals several kilometers long were used to irrigate the vast cornfields outside the city. These canals were often equipped with dams and retention basins that regulated the flow of water, enabling controlled irrigation and preventing flooding. This precise water management was essential to maintain regular harvests and support the growing population of Mayan cities.

The sophistication of Mayan irrigation systems illustrates their deep understanding of ecology and natural resource management. These techniques enabled them not only to thrive in harsh environments, but also to build flourishing civilizations based on sustainable agriculture.

Fact 46 - Mayan boats were used for maritime trade

The Maya used boats for maritime trade, playing a crucial role in the exchange of goods across the coasts of the Caribbean Sea and along inland rivers. These boats, generally canoes carved from tree trunks, were robust enough to carry goods over long distances. They sailed not only along coasts but also across larger bodies of water, linking Mayan cities to other Mesoamerican cultures. Maritime trade was essential for the supply of luxury goods such as jade, cocoa and shellfish, resources that were not always available locally.

Maya boats were adapted to a variety of navigation conditions, whether on calm rivers or on the high seas. The largest canoes could carry several passengers and considerable cargoes, making large-scale trade possible. Mayan navigators were well acquainted with ocean currents and the stars, using their knowledge to navigate at night or during less favorable seasons. They travelled well-established sea routes, creating trade networks that linked different city-states and stimulated regional economies.

Maritime trade also enabled the Maya to forge political and cultural links with other civilizations. For example, exchanges with the Toltecs and the civilizations of the Gulf of Mexico brought new ideas, technologies and artistic influences, enriching Mayan culture. Artefacts such as quetzal feathers, copper axes and fine ceramics traveled these maritime routes, testifying to the richness and diversity of the exchanges. Trading ports, such as Cancún, were dynamic places where merchants, diplomats and explorers met.

Boats were also used to transport heavy building materials such as stone blocks and wood, needed for the construction of large temples and palaces in coastal cities. Boats thus facilitated the Maya's urban and architectural development by giving them access to distant natural resources. For example, the large stone stelae found in cities such as Tulum show that maritime transport was an essential component of Mayan logistics, linking stone quarries to construction sites.

The archaeological remains of these boats, as well as the descriptions left by early Spanish explorers, illustrate the importance of Maya craft in trade and the expansion of their influence. These boats were used not only for trade, but also for fishing and ritual navigation, reflecting their versatile role in Maya society.

Fact 47 - Natural dyes colored their clothes

The Maya used natural dyes to color their garments, exploiting the riches of nature to create vibrantly colored fabrics. They had developed sophisticated techniques for extracting pigments from plants, minerals and even insects. Colorful garments were not only decorative; they also carried social, spiritual and symbolic meanings. Colors could indicate social rank, profession or role in rituals, and each hue was carefully chosen for its symbolism and cultural significance.

One of the most famous dyes used by the Maya was cochineal red, obtained from parasitic insects living on cacti. These insects were harvested, dried and crushed to produce an intense red powder used to dye textiles. This red dye was highly prized not only by the Mayans, but also by other Mesoamerican civilizations. It was often reserved for the clothing of nobles and priests, as it symbolized power and vitality. Subsequently, cochineal red became a valuable export product, attesting to its high value.

To obtain blue hues, the Mayans used a plant called indigo, which produced a long-lasting, wash-resistant color. Mayan blue, in particular, was a pigment prized for its depth and stability, even in the extreme climatic conditions of the tropics. This blue was often associated with the rain divinity, Chaac, and was found in clothing worn during rituals dedicated to rain and fertility. The complexity of indigo preparation shows the extent to which the Maya mastered the art of dyeing, combining chemical techniques with botanical knowledge.

Yellow, another popular color, was obtained from safflower, a flower whose petals produce a bright dye. Yellow symbolized light, wealth and abundance, and was often used for clothing worn at festivities and celebrations. Green, on the other hand, was made by mixing plant pigments with clay and other minerals. This mixture produced a unique hue that represented nature and regeneration, essential values in Mayan cosmology.

The Maya dyed not only their clothing, but also decorative fabrics and banners used in ceremonies. Colorful textiles were an integral part of their cultural identity, and each pattern and color carried a particular story or meaning. Archaeologists have found fragments of dyed fabrics in the tombs and ruins of ancient cities, revealing the importance of these textiles in the daily and spiritual lives of the Maya.

Fact 48 - Medicinal gardens were common among the Mayans

The Maya maintained medicinal gardens in their cities and villages, exploiting the wealth of local plants to treat a multitude of ailments. Carefully tended by healers and community sages, these gardens were essential to Mayan medicine, which was based on an in-depth knowledge of the healing properties of plants. Each garden was a veritable living laboratory, where plants with soothing, antiseptic or energizing properties were cultivated and used to prepare natural remedies.

Among the plants most commonly found in Mayan medicinal gardens was aloe vera, used for its soothing and healing properties, particularly effective against burns and cuts. Copalchi, a shrub whose bark was boiled to treat fevers, was also a must. The Maya also knew how to use plants such as mint for digestive disorders and holy basil to calm the spirits and purify the air, demonstrating a holistic approach to health that combined body and mind.

These gardens were not only places for physical healing, but also for connecting with spiritual forces. The Maya believed that each plant had a soul and a particular energy, and that caring for these plants enhanced their medicinal efficacy. The rituals surrounding the harvesting of plants were as important as their use: healers often performed prayers and offerings before picking the plants, asking permission from the spirits of nature and giving thanks for the benefits offered.

Mayan botanical knowledge was passed down from generation to generation, often orally, although some recipes and practices were engraved on codexes or steles. This transmission preserved a rich tradition of natural healing adapted to the local environment. Healers, called "aj-men" in Mayan, played a central role in society, not only by curing illness, but also by maintaining harmony between humans and their environment. They knew exactly which plants to use and how to combine them to treat specific ailments, such as infections, inflammation or joint pain.

Today, Mayan medicinal gardens continue to inspire modern herbalists and those seeking to rediscover more natural healing methods.

Fact 49 - Mayan frescoes used to decorate important buildings

Mayan frescoes were much more than mere decorations; they played an essential role in transmitting the history, culture and religious beliefs of the Mayan civilization. These works of art adorned the walls of temples, palaces and public buildings, offering visitors a vibrant glimpse into mythological stories, sacred rituals and important historical events. Each fresco was meticulously hand-painted, using natural pigments extracted from minerals and plants to create vibrant colors that have defied the centuries.

One of the most famous frescoes can be found at Bonampak, an archaeological site in the jungles of Chiapas, Mexico. These frescoes cover the walls of several temple rooms and depict scenes of battle, ceremony and celebration, illustrating the power and grandeur of Mayan rulers. The figures depicted are richly dressed, with elaborate headdresses and colorful garments, and each scene is filled with vivid details that provide insight into the complexity of Mayan society. These murals also show the importance of ritual and warfare in Mayan culture, with scenes of captured prisoners and offerings made to the gods.

The frescoes were created using sophisticated techniques that demonstrated the skill of Mayan artists. They would apply a layer of stucco to the walls before painting, creating a smooth, white surface that enhanced the colors. The pigments used, such as Mayan blue, were not only aesthetically remarkable, but also durable, resisting the humidity and heat of the tropics. This durability has enabled many frescoes to survive to the present day, providing a valuable testimony to Mayan art and culture.

In addition to their artistic value, frescoes also served to reinforce the authority of rulers and priests. They often depicted kings in majestic poses, surrounded by gods and symbols of power, such as jaguars or feathered snakes. These images reinforced the idea that kings were intermediaries between humans and deities, invested with divine power to govern their people. Frescoes could also show scenes of coronation or succession, underlining the importance of the royal lineage and the continuity of power.

Mayan frescoes were not limited to grandiose representations; they also included scenes of everyday life, such as meal preparation, dancing and the market, offering a valuable insight into ordinary Mayan life.

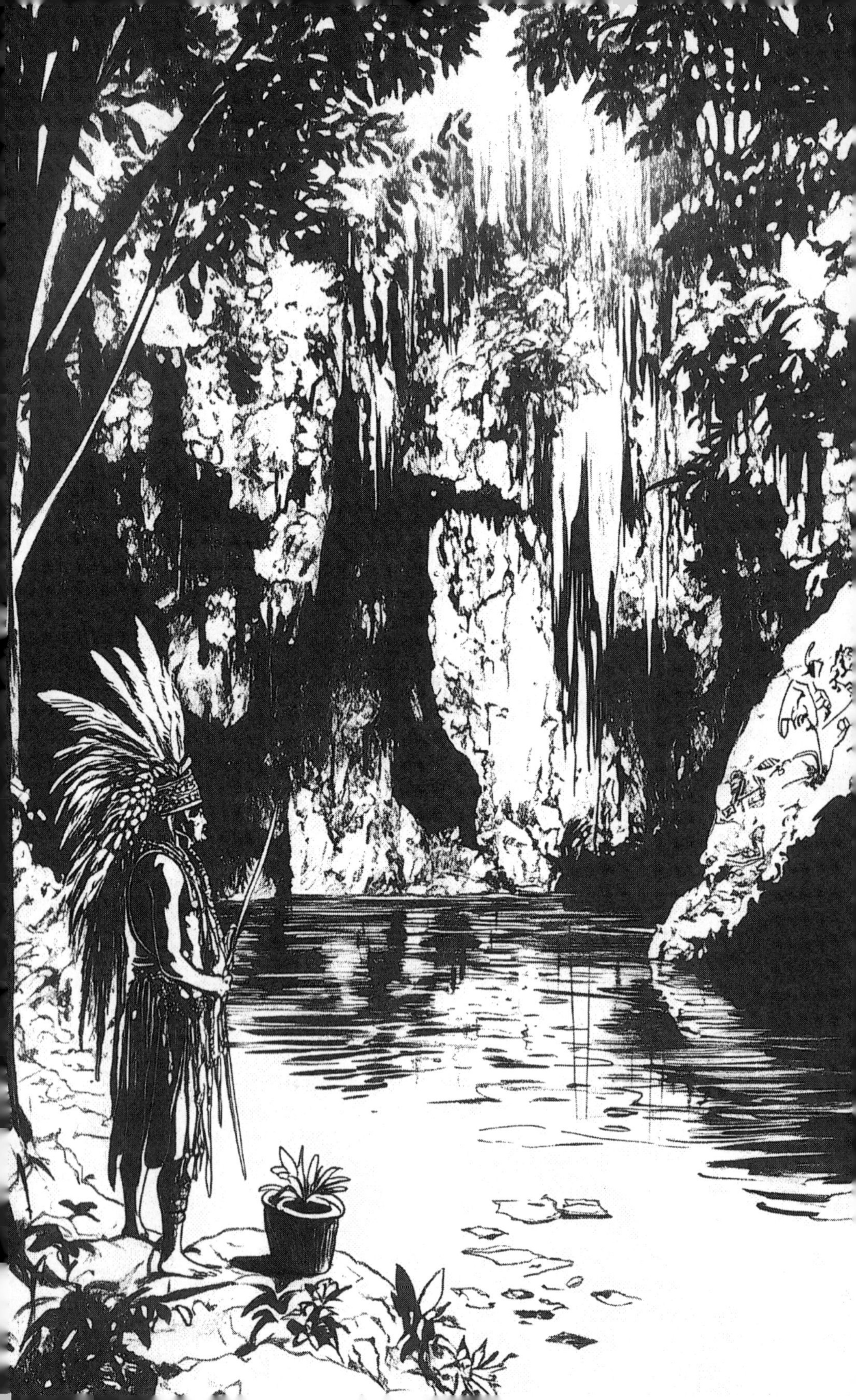

Fact 50 - The cenotes were sacred wells for the Mayas

Cenotes, natural wells formed by the collapse of freshwater-filled limestone caverns, were central to Mayan life. For them, these cavities were much more than sources of drinking water: they represented gateways to the underworld, the Xibalba, considered to be the realm of gods and spirits. The Maya saw the cenotes as sacred places, where the terrestrial world and the underworld came together, and where water, the vital element, embodied the link between life and the afterlife.

Rituals linked to the cenotes were often religious in nature, involving offerings to appease the gods, particularly Chaac, the god of rain. Archaeological excavations in famous cenotes, such as the Sacred Cenote in Chichen Itza, have revealed precious objects such as gold, ceramics and even human remains, suggesting that sacrifices were sometimes offered to obtain divine favor. These offerings were intended to ensure prosperous harvests, healthy inhabitants and protection against natural disasters, demonstrating the importance of cenotes in Mayan cosmology and daily life.

Cenotes also served as landmarks and community centers in Maya cities. Because of their abundance in the Yucatán region, the Maya often built their cities close to these freshwater wells, essential for survival in an environment that was often dry and unsuitable for agriculture without irrigation. The cenotes provided a constant source of drinking water, essential to the life of the cities, making them strategic locations not only for religion but also for the daily sustenance of the communities.

In addition to their role in ritual and water supply, cenotes were also places of legend and myth. They were often surrounded by stories about the spirits and mystical creatures that inhabited them. The Maya believed that these spirits could bring blessings or curses, depending on how they were honored or neglected. This mystical dimension reinforced respect and awe for the cenotes, prompting the Maya to treat them with great reverence and respect the rules and traditions associated with their use.

The cenotes continue to be revered today, not only by Mayan descendants, but also by those who recognize their historical and ecological value. These sacred wells still offer a fascinating insight into how the Maya understood and interacted with their environment. Their role in Mayan cultural, spiritual and practical practices shows just how deeply water, and the places that contain it, were embedded in the lives of this complex and ingenious civilization.

Fact 51 - Mayan ritual dances honored the gods

Ritual dances occupied a central place in the spiritual life of the Maya, serving to honor the gods, mark the cycles of time, and celebrate important events. These dances were not mere entertainments; they were sacred acts, deeply rooted in Mayan cosmology. Every movement, costume and instrument used in these dances had a particular meaning, representing elements of nature, divinities or mythological events. Dancers often embodied gods or spirits, playing symbolic roles to establish a link between the human and divine worlds.

During major ceremonies, dances were performed in city squares, in front of temples or around pyramids. The dancers wore richly decorated costumes, adorned with feathers, pearls and masks, often inspired by sacred animals such as the jaguar or the snake. The flamboyant costumes and rhythmic movements were accompanied by percussion, conches and chants, creating an immersive atmosphere that captured the essence of the ritual. For example, the Jaguar dance paid homage to this powerful feline, symbol of strength and connection with the underworld, while the Sun dance celebrated the solar god Kinich Ahau.

Dances also had a social and educational role, strengthening community unity and teaching myths and cultural values. Young people were often introduced to these dances at an early age, learning the steps and songs from their elders. Choreography could be complex, requiring perfect synchronization and a precise knowledge of rhythms and symbols. The transmission of these dances through the generations ensured the preservation of traditions and the continuity of religious practices, even in the face of challenges and social change.

In times of crisis, such as periods of drought or epidemics, ritual dances took on even greater importance. They were used to implore the help of the gods, seek blessings or chase away evil spirits. Specific dances, such as those dedicated to Chaac, the god of rain, were performed to request rainfall and ensure the fertility of the land. These rituals, often accompanied by prayers and offerings, demonstrated the Maya's unshakeable faith in the gods' ability to influence human destiny.

Today, Mayan ritual dances are still practiced by Mayan descendants, who continue to perform them at traditional festivals and celebrations. These dances are not just a cultural heritage; they are a living link to a rich and spiritually profound past.

Fact 52 - The Mayans invented underground irrigation systems

Faced with the challenges imposed by their environment, the Maya demonstrated remarkable ingenuity in developing sophisticated underground irrigation systems. These structures enabled them to efficiently capture and manage water, essential for their crops in regions often marked by prolonged dry seasons. The Maya dug underground canals and built reservoirs, called chultuns, to store rainwater and feed their fields in times of drought. These innovations demonstrate their ability to adapt their agriculture to difficult environmental conditions.

Chultuns were cavities dug into the limestone, lined with stucco to prevent water from seeping into the ground. They functioned as cisterns capable of holding thousands of liters of water, ensuring a reserve in case of need. These reservoirs were often linked to a network of canals that distributed water directly to the crops, enabling the Maya to maintain stable agricultural production even when rainfall was insufficient. This ingenious approach shows how the Maya used their knowledge of the terrain to maximize the use of available resources.

Underground canals were sometimes complemented by natural filter systems, using layers of sand and gravel to purify the water before it reached the fields. This technique improved water quality, reducing risks to crops and increasing yields. The Maya understood the importance of preserving the integrity of their water resources, enabling them to support large populations in their city-states. The remains of these irrigation systems bear witness to their technical know-how and their ability to anticipate future needs.

A striking example of this hydraulic engineering can be found at Tikal, where archaeologists have uncovered a complex network of underground canals and reservoirs. These installations were not only agricultural tools, but also strategic elements in the city's urban organization. The canals not only ensured irrigation, but also served to drain excess water during heavy rains, thus preventing flooding. This mastery of water not only demonstrated the ingenuity of the Maya, but also their ability to incorporate practical solutions into the design of their cities.

The success of these underground irrigation systems is even more impressive when you consider that they were designed and implemented without modern technology.

Fact 53 - The Mayans predicted the weather by observing the sky

The Mayans possessed an advanced knowledge of astronomy and used this expertise to predict weather conditions. By carefully observing the movements of the stars, planets and especially the Sun and Moon, they were able to predict rainy seasons, periods of drought and even specific climatic events. Their understanding of celestial cycles enabled them to adapt their agriculture and plan sowing and harvesting according to weather forecasts.

Astronomical priests, known as ah k'in, played a key role in these forecasts. They spent entire nights observing the stars from high platforms, noting the positions of celestial bodies and comparing them with ancient calendars and astronomical tables engraved on monuments. By analyzing the appearances and disappearances of constellations, as well as the positions of Venus and other planets, the Maya were able to interpret the signs in the sky to predict future weather changes. For example, the appearance of certain stars at dawn heralded the start of the rainy season, essential for agriculture.

The Maya also paid close attention to atmospheric phenomena, such as the colors of the sky at sunrise and sunset, and the shapes and movements of clouds. These observations enabled them to detect variations in climatic conditions, such as impending storms or wind changes. The Maya understood that the sky's behavior was intimately linked to terrestrial events, and saw these signs as divine messages. This belief reinforced the importance of weather predictions in their culture and daily life.

A fascinating aspect of their knowledge was their ability to associate eclipses and other celestial events with climatic changes. The Maya saw solar and lunar eclipses as warning signs, potentially heralding natural disasters such as prolonged droughts. For them, the sky was a living map, rich in symbols and meaning, and celestial phenomena were interpreted through the prism of their cosmology. This vision of the world enabled them to adapt their actions according to the forecasts, from protection rituals to agricultural adjustments.

The knowledge accumulated over generations was carefully preserved in codices, where priests recorded meteorological and astronomical data.

Fact 54 - Mayan markets were lively and well organized

Mayan markets were central to daily life, where activity was in full swing. These spaces teemed with merchants, customers and products ranging from fresh foods to colorful textiles. They were often located near the main plazas of the city-states, as in Chichén Itzá or Tikal. The market was not only a place of commercial exchange, but also a social center where Mayans gathered to discuss, negotiate and exchange news.

The organization of Mayan markets was surprisingly well structured. Spaces were divided into specialized sections, each dedicated to specific products such as ceramics, clothing, tools or food. Archaeologists have uncovered the remains of stone platforms and stalls, indicating a carefully planned layout. Merchants occupied fixed locations, and customers knew exactly where to find the products they needed. This organization facilitated trade and made the market efficient and dynamic.

The markets offered a wide variety of goods from different regions, reflecting the extent of the Maya trade network. Products such as cocoa, corn, salt, honey and quetzal feathers, highly prized for the clothing of the elite, were traded. Seashells and obsidians, brought from afar, testified to the extensive trade links between the Maya and other Mesoamerican civilizations. This diversity of products created a vibrant and animated environment, where colors, sounds and smells mingled to captivate all the senses.

Market transactions were not carried out with money as we know it today, but by bartering or using high-value goods such as cocoa or specific shellfish. The Maya had developed a very precise value system for each product, enabling fair and balanced exchanges. Merchants were experts in the art of negotiation, and it was not uncommon to see heated discussions about the value of a good. This economy based on barter and the intrinsic value of objects required a great deal of product knowledge and negotiation skills.

Markets were also places of entertainment and ritual. Musicians, dancers and storytellers enlivened market days, adding a festive dimension to the shopping experience. Rituals and ceremonies in honor of the gods of trade and prosperity could also take place in the markets, reinforcing the importance of these places in Mayan culture.

Fact 55 - Mayan cities had different levels and structures

Maya cities were masterpieces of architecture and engineering, characterized by varied structures and levels that reflected a complex social and religious organization. Each city was unique, but all shared a hierarchy of spaces, with central squares, pyramidal temples, palaces and residential quarters organized in distinct levels. The main squares were used for rituals and public gatherings, while the temples and pyramids, often located high up, symbolized the power of the elite and proximity to the gods.

The varied levels of Mayan cities were not simply aesthetic, but served specific functions. At Tikal, for example, temples and palaces were built on terraces and elevated plateaus, giving a commanding view of the surrounding jungle. These levels also served to separate social functions: the higher areas were often reserved for the elite and religious activities, while the lower levels housed markets, communal dwellings and craft production areas.

The tiered organization also had a practical aspect, particularly in tropical environments where water and erosion management were essential. The Maya designed complex drainage and water retention systems, integrated into the very structures of their cities. Terraces, for example, were not just spaces for buildings, but played a role in managing rainwater, preventing flooding and soil erosion. This environmental engineering testified to their in-depth knowledge of the landscape and their sophisticated adaptation techniques.

Mayan cities were also adorned with sculptures, stelae and frescoes decorating the various levels, recounting the exploits of kings and gods. These visual elements served to reinforce the importance of sacred places and remind inhabitants of the link between rulers and the divine. The upper levels, where the elite lived and ceremonies took place, were often the most lavishly decorated, displaying symbols of power and prestige that underlined the hierarchy of Mayan society.

Finally, each city was designed with a precise cosmic alignment, often oriented according to the movements of stars such as the Sun and Venus. This alignment reinforced the importance of the levels and structures, connecting them directly to Mayan religious beliefs and complex calendars. The cities, with their varied levels and elaborate structures, thus represented a perfect fusion of architecture, nature and spirituality, creating urban environments that continued to reflect the cosmic and terrestrial order essential to Mayan civilization.

Fact 56 - Bone instruments created the music for ceremonies

The Maya had a rich musical tradition, incorporating a variety of instruments to accompany their religious ceremonies and rituals. Among these instruments, bone flutes and whistles figured prominently. Made from the bones of animals such as deer and birds, these instruments produced unique sounds that resonated during rituals, reinforcing the mystical and sacred atmosphere. Each instrument was carefully carved and sometimes decorated with engravings depicting religious or symbolic motifs, underlining their role in spiritual practices.

These bone instruments were not only used to create music, but also to communicate with gods and spirits. The sounds produced by these flutes and whistles were considered divine voices, capable of crossing the terrestrial and spiritual worlds. Priests and shamans often used them to invoke deities or guide souls into the afterlife. This use of sound in a sacred context demonstrates the importance of music in Mayan cosmology and their belief in the power of sound to influence the spiritual world.

The manufacture of bone instruments required great expertise. Craftsmen had to carefully select the bones, prepare them through a process of cleaning and polishing, then drill and carve them with precision to create the desired tones. This process could include adding extra holes to adjust the notes, or engraving patterns to reinforce the instrument's spiritual connection. Each flute or whistle was unique, not only in its material but also in the sound it produced, reflecting the individuality of the ceremonies for which it was used.

Music played on these bone instruments was often accompanied by other ritual sounds, such as drums or conches, creating a sacred symphony that enveloped participants in an atmosphere of devotion. These compositions were not simply artistic performances; they served to punctuate rituals, to mark key moments in ceremonies, and to help participants enter a trance or connect with divine energies. The role of music went far beyond mere entertainment, acting as a bridge between humans and higher forces.

Archaeological discoveries of these instruments, found in tombs or near temples, attest to their importance in the daily and spiritual life of the Maya. They are silent witnesses to a time when every sound had a profound meaning, and when music was an essential tool for navigating between the visible and invisible worlds.

Fact 57 - The Maya wove intricately patterned garments

The Maya were masters of weaving, and their garments were distinguished by highly complex patterns. The weaving process was an art passed down from generation to generation, mainly among women. They used belt looms, a simple but effective tool, to create textiles with geometric patterns, religious symbols and representations of nature. Each motif had a precise meaning, often linked to spiritual beliefs or the identity of the wearer.

Textiles were mainly made from cotton fibers, which the Mayans grew and harvested themselves. The cotton was then spun into fine threads and dyed with natural dyes extracted from plants, animals and minerals. These natural dyes, such as indigo for blue or red from cochineal, were used to create a palette of vibrant colors. The know-how of dyers was crucial to obtaining uniform, resistant shades, contributing to the longevity of garments.

Woven garments were not only used to protect against the weather or to cover the body, they were also a means of social expression. Patterns and colors could indicate a person's social status, wealth, or even ritual function. The elite wore garments adorned with feathers, jade or shells, incorporating elements that reflected their power and proximity to the gods. By contrast, the clothing of the lower classes, though simpler, always showed great care in the choice of patterns and colors.

The process of creating these textiles required not only time, but also great skill. Weaving could take weeks or even months, depending on the complexity of the pattern and the size of the garment. Craftsmen worked meticulously, line by line, adjusting each thread to form precise patterns. This patience and precision reflect not only the skill of the weavers, but also the cultural importance of textiles in Mayan society.

Textiles woven by the Maya were so precious that they were sometimes used as currency. They were offered in homage to the gods or used in important commercial transactions. Far from being simple everyday objects, the garments were in fact wearable works of art, celebrating the cultural richness of the Maya. Today, these weaving techniques continue to inspire many indigenous communities, preserving the heritage of this age-old art.

Fact 58 - The Mayans had balanced diets

The Maya were renowned for their varied, well-balanced diet, which reflected both their agricultural ingenuity and their understanding of natural resources. Their staple diet relied heavily on maize, considered not only an essential foodstuff, but also a sacred gift from the gods. Corn was transformed into tortillas, tamales and atoles, providing the energy needed to sustain their active lifestyle and daily activities.

In addition to corn, the Mayans consumed beans and squash, creating an essential food trio, often referred to as "the three sisters". This combination offered a perfect balance of protein, carbohydrates and fiber, helping to maintain a healthy diet. Beans were a major source of protein, while squash provided important vitamins and minerals. The Mayans intuitively understood the importance of combining these foods to obtain a complete diet.

The Maya also incorporated a variety of fruits and vegetables grown in their gardens or gathered from the wild into their diet. Fruits such as avocados, papayas and guavas enriched their diet with vitamins, while leafy greens, chillies and tubers further diversified their meals. The use of chillies and spices, such as coriander and epazote, not only enhanced the taste of dishes, but also played a role in preserving food and promoting digestion.

Meat occupied a more modest place in the Maya diet, but was not absent. They hunted wild animals such as deer, turkeys and peccaries, and also raised domestic dogs and turkeys. Rivers and lakes provided them with fish and other aquatic products, adding further sources of protein and essential nutrients. The Maya also knew how to smoke or salt meat to preserve it longer, enabling them to incorporate it into their diet on a more regular basis.

Finally, the Maya understood the importance of nutritious drinks, such as cocoa, which, when mixed with spices or corn, became a highly appreciated energy drink. They also drank pinole, a ground corn-based beverage, and various herbal infusions. These beverages complemented their diet, providing not only extra calories but also gustatory pleasure, while reinforcing their connection with nature and their spiritual beliefs. Thanks to this dietary diversity, the Mayans were able to maintain a balanced diet adapted to their needs, while celebrating the richness of their natural environment.

Fact 59 - Precious stones were used for divination

The Mayans, fascinated by the beauty and mystical properties of gemstones, used them not only as ornaments, but also in divinatory practices. These stones, such as jade, obsidian and quartz, were considered receptacles of divine energy and served to establish a link with the spiritual worlds. Priests and shamans used them to interpret messages from the gods and predict future events, whether to guide rulers or to allay the concerns of the people.

Jade, in particular, played a central role in divinatory rituals. In addition to its use in royal ornaments and funerary objects, jade was used to read signs and omens. Its green color was associated with life, fertility and prosperity, and its rarity made it an ideal material for attracting divine favors. During ceremonies, priests could contemplate the reflections of jade under sun or moonlight to interpret the gods' answers to questions.

Obsidian, a shiny black volcanic stone, was also prized for divination. It often served as a magic mirror, enabling shamans to see visions or hidden messages. Obsidian was used to peer into the future, but also for more down-to-earth practices such as finding clues about enemies or conspiracies. Priests cut obsidian into disks or blades, sometimes even into symbolic shapes, to maximize their power of revelation.

Quartz, translucent and often found in the form of brilliant crystals, was also a stone of choice in divinatory rituals. Considered an energy amplifier, quartz enabled priests to connect more deeply with cosmic forces. The Maya believed that quartz crystals could capture starlight and transmit it in the form of visions or signs. Rituals involving quartz could take place in caves or near water, where the energy of the natural elements further enhanced the stone's power.

Gemstone divination was not limited to predicting the future; it also played a crucial role in making important decisions, such as political alliances, military campaigns or critical moments in community life. Mayan rulers, in particular, often turned to these practices for advice on how to govern or to ensure the success of their projects. This reliance on stones to guide their actions shows the extent to which the Maya were intimately linked to nature and the forces they perceived as divine.

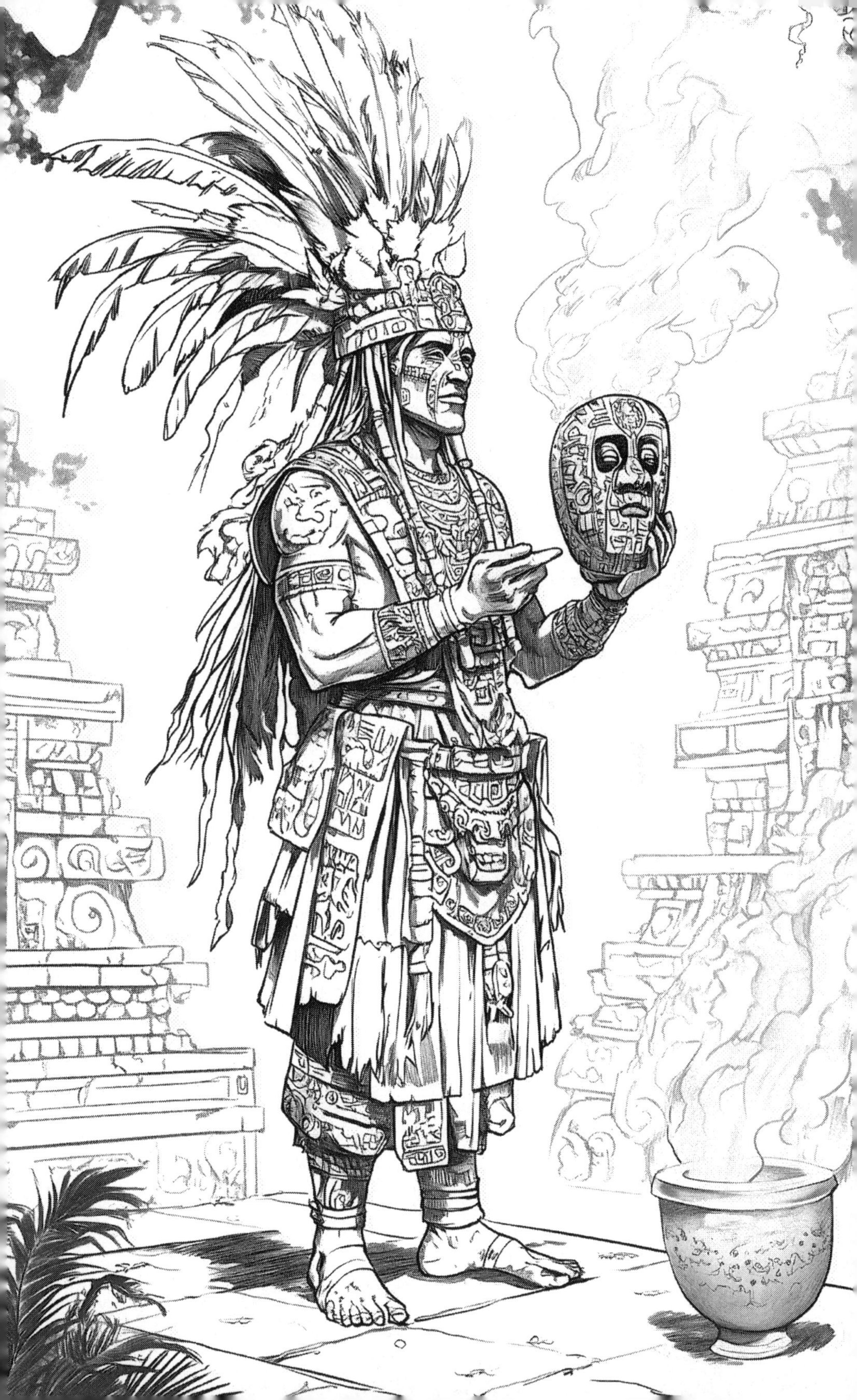

Fact 60 - Masks honored ancestors during ceremonies

The Maya had a deep respect for their ancestors, whom they regarded as protectors and spiritual guides. To honor them, they used masks in various religious and ritual ceremonies. These masks, often decorated with intricate designs and made from precious materials such as jade, obsidian or ceramics, served as a bridge between the world of the living and that of the spirits. Masks were much more than mere accessories: they embodied the soul and power of ancestors, enabling them to be invoked and their benevolence sought.

Masks representing ancestors were worn by priests and rulers during rituals marking important moments, such as coronations, weddings or harvest celebrations. Sometimes, they represented idealized faces, with exaggerated features to symbolize wisdom, strength or nobility. The art of mask-making was passed down from generation to generation, with craftsmen dedicating their lives to perfecting the techniques of carving and decoration. Each mask carried a unique story, rooted in family legends and beliefs.

The ceremonies in which these masks were used were often accompanied by ritual dances, songs and offerings designed to appease the spirits of the ancestors. Participants believed that the masks, once animated by prayers and rituals, became veritable channels of communication with the souls of the deceased. The masks not only served to pay homage to the ancestors, but also to strengthen community ties by recalling the achievements and values of past generations.

Masks could also be used to represent mythical ancestors or divine figures, often blurring the boundaries between the human and the divine. During rituals, mask wearers would assume specific postures and movements that imitated the gestures of the spirits they embodied, creating an atmosphere of mysticism and reverence. Ceremonies then became a sacred theater where the living and the dead shared a common space, where stories of the world's creation and mythical ancestors came to life before everyone's eyes.

These masks also had an educational role, passing on the stories and lessons of the ancestors to younger generations. By seeing the masks and participating in the rituals, children learned about their roots, the values of their culture, and the importance of respecting and venerating those who had gone before them. In this way, the masks did more than simply celebrate the past; they played an active role in preserving the identity and collective memory of the Maya, linking generations through time.

Fact 61 - Shuffleboard was a Mayan pastime

In addition to their ritual activities and daily life, the Maya also had times for leisure, and shuffleboard games were an integral part of their play culture. These games, similar to games of skill or precision, were often played on flat surfaces where participants sought to throw or slide shuffles towards specific targets. The pucks, made of stone, wood or bone, were often finely carved and sometimes decorated, reflecting the importance of these games in Mayan society.

Shuffleboard served not only as entertainment, but also as a means of strengthening social and community ties. They were played at family gatherings, community festivals, and sometimes even in temple courtyards, underlining their role in social interaction. The rules of these games varied from region to region, but the main objective remained precision and skill, qualities particularly prized by the Maya. Some games required strategic skills, urging participants to anticipate their opponents' movements and plan their moves carefully.

These games also had a symbolic dimension, some representing aspects of Mayan cosmology, such as cycles of time or celestial movements. For example, concentric circles or spiral patterns could symbolize the movement of the sun or planets, recalling the importance of astronomical observation in Mayan culture. Thus, playing these games was not just a pastime, but also a way of connecting with the sacred elements of their beliefs.

The competitive aspect of shuffleboard was also a way for young warriors and other community members to demonstrate their dexterity and ability to stay focused under pressure. In some regions, official competitions were organized, attracting enthusiastic spectators who came to cheer on their champions. These events reinforced a sense of belonging and local pride, while offering a welcome break from the demands of everyday life.

Finally, shuffleboard was also passed down from generation to generation, with the elders teaching the young not only the rules, but also the values of respect, patience and fair play. These moments of transmission were an opportunity to share stories, anecdotes and life lessons, deeply rooting shuffleboard in Mayan tradition and cultural heritage. This pastime, more than just fun, played a key role in the education and cohesion of Mayan society.

Fact 62 - Rituals marked royal births

Among the Maya, the birth of a royal child was an event of major importance, surrounded by sacred rituals and ceremonies designed to secure the blessing of the gods. These rituals were designed to protect the child, ensure his or her health and prepare him or her for the future as a ruler. From the moment of birth, the royal newborn was regarded as a being endowed with a divine connection, embodying both hope and the continuity of the royal lineage.

Priests played a central role in these rituals, performing incantations and prayers to invoke the protection of the gods over the child and his family. Ceremonies often included offerings, such as feathers, jade or precious incense, placed on altars specially erected for the occasion. These offerings symbolized the royal family's devotion to the deities and their wish for prosperity and longevity for the newborn.

A common practice at royal births was to consult astrologers, who analyzed the stars and celestial cycles to determine the child's destiny. The Maya firmly believed that the positions of the stars at the moment of birth could influence the individual's future life. Thus, astrological predictions helped shape decisions concerning the education, alliances and even future political roles of young royalty.

The ritual bath was another essential component of royal birth rituals. The bath symbolized the child's purification and preparation for his or her future life. The water used in this ritual was often collected from sacred springs or cenotes, places considered to be passageways to the underworld. The participation of royal parents and influential members of the court reinforced the importance of this ceremony, marking the child with sacred protection and authority.

Finally, naming ceremonies followed the ritual bath, where the child's name was carefully chosen to reflect the aspirations and values of the royal family. This name often carried significance linked to historical events, illustrious ancestors or desired qualities. The Maya believed that the name influenced not only the child's identity, but also his or her future role in society. The complex rituals surrounding royal births highlighted the importance of lineage and tradition in Mayan culture, where each new life was seen as a living link between past, present and future.

Fact 63 - Skin drums were part of Mayan ceremonies

Skin drums played a crucial role in Mayan ceremonies, creating rhythms that echoed through temples and public squares. These instruments were often made from animal skins stretched over wooden frames, producing deep, powerful sounds. The beating of the drums was seen as a way of communicating with the gods and honoring ancestral spirits, their repetitive rhythm facilitating the trance of participants during rituals.

Religious ceremonies and community festivals were punctuated by these drums, which symbolized the connection between humans and the divine. Priests and musicians, often from families specializing in the art of percussion, played the drums to accompany sacred chants and ritual dances. Their mastery of the instruments enabled them to vary the rhythms according to the type of ceremony, whether it was a tribute to the rain gods, a harvest celebration or a rite of passage.

Drums were also used to mark time and structure complex ceremonies, such as sacrifices or invocations. Their deep resonance was supposed to imitate thunder, a natural phenomenon often associated with divine power. The rhythm of the drums guided the dancers' movements, coordinating their steps and symbolic gestures in perfect harmony with other ritual elements, such as incense and offerings.

Sometimes, drums were decorated with symbolic motifs depicting deities, sacred animals or mythological scenes, adding a visual dimension to their sonic presence. These decorations were not only aesthetic, they also carried religious significance, reinforcing the instrument's spiritual power. Playing a drum decorated with sacred symbols was perceived as an act of devotion, each stroke of the drumstick being a sonic offering to supernatural forces.

The importance of drums in Mayan culture went beyond religious ceremonies; they were also used to transmit messages over long distances, their echoes echoing signals between different parts of the city-states. This ability to communicate through sound reinforced drums' role as instruments of power and connection, linking communities and gods through a ritual symphony where each beat told an ancestral story.

Fact 64 - Agricultural activities were guided by lunar cycles

The Maya carefully observed lunar cycles to plan their agricultural activities, closely linking astronomy to their daily way of life. The Moon, with its changing phases, was seen as a natural guide for deciding when to sow, harvest and even chop wood. Each phase had a particular meaning: for example, the new moon was often associated with the start of sowing, symbolizing a new beginning for crops.

Knowledge of lunar cycles was passed down from generation to generation, often through the astronomical priests who kept precise records of these observations. Thanks to their expertise, these specialists were able to advise farmers on the best times to plant corn, a central component of the Mayan diet. They believed that certain lunar phases favored plant growth, while other periods were less beneficial.

The lunar influence was not limited to the fields; it also dictated the appropriate times for agricultural rituals. The Maya held ceremonies on full moons to implore the favor of the gods, hoping for abundant harvests. These rituals often included food offerings and prayers for beneficial rains. In this way, the Moon became a tangible link between human needs and cosmic forces.

Observing the Moon also enabled the Maya to mark time seasonally. By following the progression of lunar cycles, they could predict climatic changes and adapt their agricultural practices accordingly. For example, they knew that certain lunar periods preceded the rainy seasons, crucial for crop development. This advance knowledge of climatic conditions gave them an advantage in optimizing their harvests.

This lunar approach reflected a worldview in which agriculture and astronomy were inextricably linked, underlining the harmony the Maya sought to maintain with nature. Each cultivated field was not simply a plot of land, but a space where celestial cycles dictated the rhythm of agricultural work. This respect for natural cycles demonstrated their deep attachment to the balance between earth and sky, a fundamental principle of their civilization.

Fact 65 - Mayan frescoes celebrated great victories

Mayan frescoes were much more than simple wall decorations: they served as veritable visual chronicles of the military exploits and glorious victories of city-states. These works of art, often found in temples and palaces, depicted scenes of battles, captives and triumphs, immortalizing moments of glory for rulers and warriors alike. They celebrated the power of the city and reminded inhabitants and enemies alike of the strength and bravery of the Maya.

Each fresco was rich in detail, using natural pigments to create vibrant, dynamic images. Mayan artists, whose work was highly respected, depicted warriors in action, brandishing their weapons and wearing elaborate costumes that emphasized their rank and success. These frescoes not only depicted the violence of combat, but also included symbolic elements such as gods and mythical creatures, underlining the divine support assumed in these conflicts.

A striking example can be found in the frescoes of Bonampak, a Mayan city famous for its depictions of battle scenes and post-victory celebrations. These frescoes show not only soldiers in battle, but also defeated captives, illustrating the fate reserved for enemies. Images of victorious warriors offer a glimpse of the rituals that followed battles, including dances and offerings, marking victory not only as a military feat, but also as a deeply spiritual event.

Frescoes also served to reinforce the authority of kings and nobles, who often appeared at the center of these representations, crowned with their sumptuous headdresses and surrounded by their courtiers. The frescoes presented them not only as military leaders, but also as divine figures, uniting earth and heaven. They played a key role in political propaganda, consolidating the power of the elites and inspiring loyalty and admiration among the population.

As well as celebrating past victories, the frescoes had an educational function, reminding future generations of the great deeds of their ancestors. They were a powerful means of transmitting Mayan history, culture and martial values. By observing these frescoes, young warriors learned the stories of courage and sacrifice that defined their civilization, reinforcing their sense of duty and courage in defending their city.

Fact 66 - The Maya carved obelisks to make history

The Maya used obelisks, also known as stelae, to immortalize key events in their history. These tall stone structures served as veritable stone books, recounting military victories, political alliances and key moments in the lives of kings and nobles. They were often placed in public squares or in front of temples, visible to all, constantly reminding inhabitants and visitors of the importance of the events recorded.

The stelae were carved with great precision and ornamentation, adorned with hieroglyphs and engraved images describing the exploits of the kings. These inscriptions not only described the facts, but also included precise dates, thanks to the use of the Mayan calendar to situate events in time. This dating method was so precise that modern archaeologists can reconstruct detailed chronologies of Mayan history from these stelae.

An outstanding example is Stele 31 at Tikal, which commemorates the victories of King Siyaj Chan K'awiil II. This monument not only glorifies the king's military successes, but also represents his rise to power and his role in consolidating the dynasty. The images show the king in heroic poses, surrounded by symbols of power, reinforcing his divine status and uncontested authority over his subjects.

Stelae were not only tools of political propaganda; they also served as cultural and spiritual landmarks. By engraving important events on these obelisks, the Maya believed they were establishing a lasting link between the terrestrial and spiritual worlds. Each stele acted as a bridge between generations, allowing ancestors to be honored and lessons from the past to be passed on.

In carving obelisks, the Maya sought not only to preserve their stories for themselves, but also to send a message to future generations. Every engraving, every hieroglyph on these monuments was a declaration of their greatness and resilience, an affirmation of their identity as a sophisticated civilization proud of its heritage. These monuments, standing despite the centuries, continue to speak of Mayan greatness, offering a lasting testimony to their rich and complex history.

Fact 67 - The Maya had rare zoos

The Maya, fascinated by nature and the animal world, created zoological gardens where they gathered rare and exotic creatures. These areas, often located close to royal residences and temples, served both to demonstrate the power of the rulers and to honor animals regarded as divine symbols. Jaguars, spider monkeys and colorful birds such as quetzals were among the most prized collections, representing spiritual or warlike aspects.

These zoos were much more than mere curiosities; they played a central role in Mayan rituals and religious beliefs. For example, jaguars, symbols of power and connection with the spirit world, were often used in ceremonies designed to invoke the protection of the gods or guarantee the prosperity of the city. Birds, with their dazzling feathers, represented the beauty of the sky and were associated with aerial divinities.

Capturing and maintaining these rare animals was no simple task, and a testament to the Maya's skill in animal care. They understood the importance of a suitable habitat, recreating natural environments in their enclosures to maintain the animals' well-being. Zoological gardens were laid out with trees, water basins and shaded areas, all to mimic the natural environment of the species housed, demonstrating their understanding of the ecological needs of each animal.

These animal collections also served as diplomatic tools and symbols of prestige. Offering a rare animal as a diplomatic gift could strengthen alliances between city-states or assert a king's dominance over a neighboring region. At Palenque, for example, inscriptions tell how exotic animals offered by neighboring chiefs symbolized recognition of the local king's power. Thus, zoological gardens were as much showcases of wealth as instruments of political power.

The existence of these zoos offers us a glimpse into the complexity and richness of Mayan civilization. They demonstrate their ability to capture, understand and integrate the natural world into their daily lives and spiritual practices. These spaces were as much a reflection of their mastery of the living world as a manifestation of their devotion to the gods, fusing nature, religion and power in one place.

Fact 68 - The Maya had food preservation methods

The Maya, with their exceptional agricultural know-how, had also developed ingenious techniques for preserving their food. These methods were essential to ensure the survival of their communities, especially during periods of drought or between harvests. Corn, a staple in their diet, was often dried and stored in raised granaries to protect it from moisture and rodents. This storage maintained the quality of the grain and prevented famine.

For fruits and vegetables, the Maya used sun-drying methods that preserved nutrients while extending shelf life. Chillies, for example, were not only dried for preservation but also to intensify their flavour, becoming a valuable resource in cooking and traditional medicine. This simple but effective technique enabled them to preserve surplus harvests and use them throughout the year.

Salting was another method used by the Mayans, particularly for meat and fish. By rubbing these foods with salt, they slowed the growth of bacteria, making them edible for extended periods. The presence of salt marshes along the coast provided an abundant source of salt, an essential element not only for food preservation, but also for trade with other city-states.

The Maya also used fermentation, a sophisticated technique for its time, to preserve and enrich certain foods. Fermented cocoa, for example, not only preserved better but also developed richer flavours, becoming a beverage prized by the elite. This method also extended to the production of fermented beverages such as balché, a sacred drink made from honey and tree bark, used during religious rituals.

These food preservation methods demonstrate the Maya's in-depth understanding of their environment and its resources. By optimizing the way they stored and preserved food, they ensured the food stability of their cities, even in the face of climatic challenges. This ingenuity reflects their ability to innovate and adapt, essential qualities that enabled their civilization to prosper for centuries.

Fact 69 - Underground reservoirs used to store water

Faced with an often hostile environment and prolonged periods of drought, the Maya developed ingenious solutions for managing water, a resource vital to their survival. One of these major innovations was the construction of underground reservoirs called chultuns. These structures, dug into the limestone rock, were designed to collect and store rainwater, providing communities with a reserve of drinking water even during the dry seasons.

These reservoirs were carefully planned and located close to urban centers, fields or temples to maximize their usefulness. Chultuns were often coated with an impermeable stucco-based coating to prevent leaks and protect the stored water from contaminants. Thanks to this technique, the Maya were able to maintain the water supply of their cities, particularly in regions where natural water sources were scarce or non-existent.

The importance of chultuns is particularly apparent in sites like Tikal, where freshwater was a precious resource. At Tikal, the Maya created a complex network of interconnected canals and reservoirs, transforming rainwater into a strategic asset for the city. This water management system reflects not only their advanced understanding of hydraulic engineering, but also their ability to adapt infrastructure to environmental challenges.

Chultuns also had a ritual dimension in some regions. Stored water was not only intended for domestic or agricultural use, but could also be used in religious ceremonies. Perceived as a blessing from the gods, water played a central role in rites of purification and renewal, integrating spiritual needs with everyday necessities.

This mastery of water resources demonstrates the ingenuity of the Maya in the face of a complex environment. By developing underground reservoirs to store rainwater, they were able to take advantage of natural elements to secure the future of their communities. These technical innovations, while meeting immediate needs, are part of a broader vision of sustainable resource management, which contributed to the longevity and prosperity of the Maya civilization.

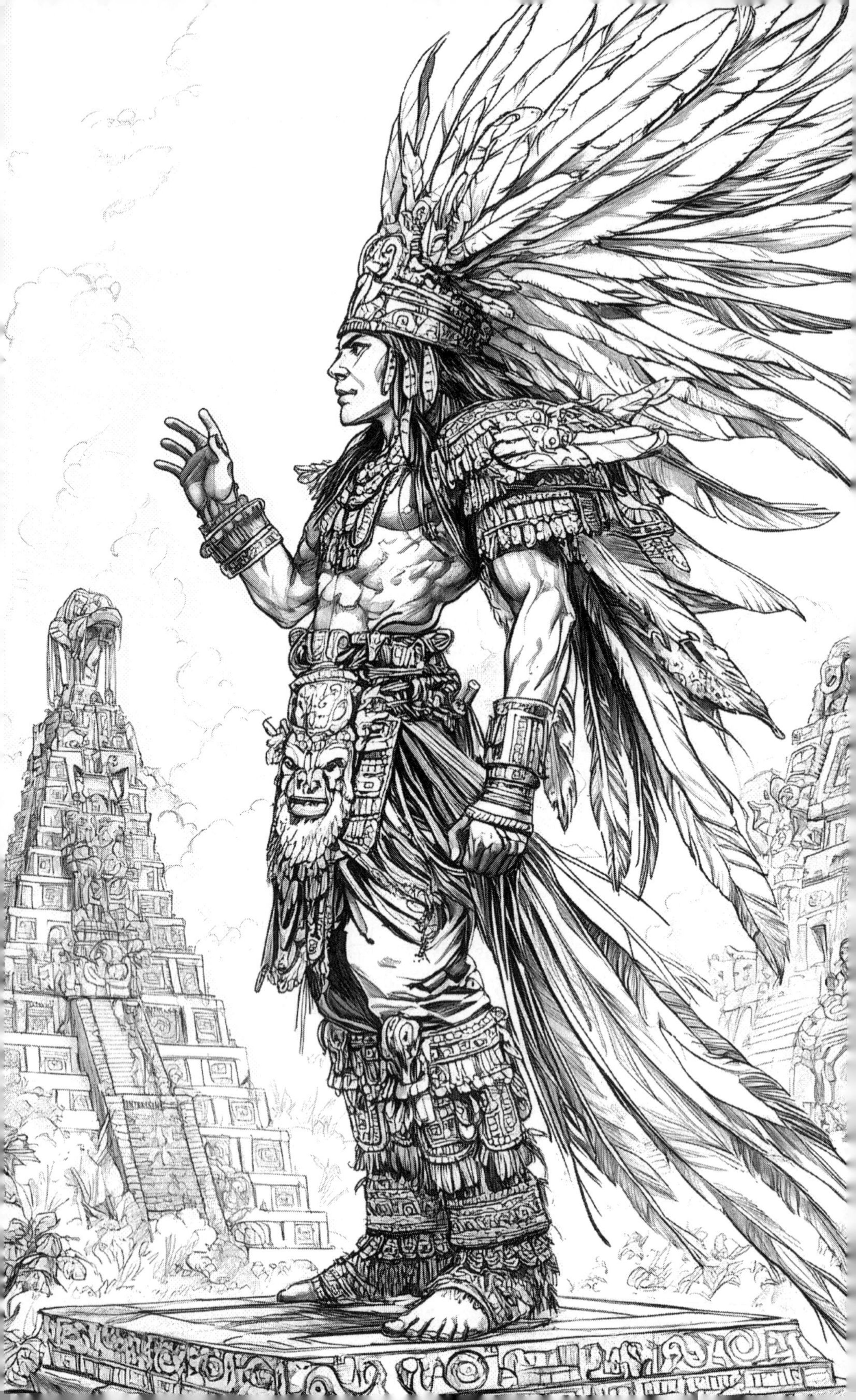

Fact 70 - Royal costumes were adorned with colorful feathers

Mayan royal costumes were true works of art, magnificently adorned with colorful feathers that symbolized wealth, power and connection with the divine. The feathers used came from exotic birds such as the quetzal, whose long green feathers were particularly prized for their rarity and brilliance. These ornaments testified to the high status of their wearers and were used to distinguish kings and nobles during important ceremonies.

These costumes were not only garments, but also symbols of divine authority. By wearing feathers, kings embodied the gods of the heavens and affirmed their role as mediators between humans and the spiritual world. The bright colors of the feathers, often combined with precious stones and richly embroidered fabrics, made the costumes even more impressive and spectacular.

Collecting feathers for these costumes was a sacred task, often reserved for specialized hunters who knew the deep forests where the rarest birds lived. These hunters not only had to capture the birds without killing them, as their lives were precious for the rituals, but also ensure that the feathers remained intact and bright. This practice underlined the importance of natural resources in Mayan culture and their respect for sacred creatures.

During major ceremonies, such as coronations or rites of passage, kings would appear in these sumptuous costumes, impressing both the people and other nobles. The spectacle of these feathered garments floating in the wind added a captivating visual dimension to the rituals, reinforcing the mystical and majestic aura of royal power. These public appearances were carefully orchestrated to recall the central role of rulers in Mayan cosmology.

Feathers were not confined to the costumes of kings; they also adorned the headdresses, shields and other accessories of the warrior and religious elites. By using these natural elements with such refinement, the Maya showed not only their artistic sense, but also their ability to integrate nature into their highest cultural expressions. Today, these costumes remain dazzling symbols of the splendor and sophistication of Mayan civilization.

Fact 71 - Mayan rituals for solar eclipses were complex

The Maya attached immense importance to solar eclipses, regarding them as fearsome cosmic events requiring precise and elaborate rituals. For them, a solar eclipse was not just an astronomical phenomenon, but a sign of imbalance in the natural order and a potential threat to the world. These events were perceived as celestial battles in which the sun was under attack, requiring human intervention to restore cosmic harmony.

To appease the gods and protect the sun, the Maya organized ceremonies rich in symbolism and ritual action. Priests, dressed in costumes adorned with feathers and jewels, played a central role, performing complex prayers and incantations. Rituals often included offerings of jade, corn and even blood sacrifices, which were supposed to nourish the gods and give them the strength to repel the dark forces threatening the sun.

These rituals took place in sacred places, such as temples dedicated to the solar god Kinich Ahau, where the community gathered to actively participate in the ceremonies. Songs and dances accompanied the rites, creating a solemn, mystical atmosphere. As eclipses were unpredictable and awe-inspiring, people's participation strengthened the link between humans and the cosmos, making these events deeply spiritual and communal.

Thanks to their advanced knowledge of celestial cycles, Mayan astrologers were sometimes able to predict eclipses, giving them an almost divine status within society. They used astronomical tables engraved on codices to anticipate these phenomena and prepare rituals in advance. This ability to predict the future of the heavens reinforced the idea that priests had direct access to the divine will, consolidating their power and influence over the people.

In addition to rituals to appease the gods, the Maya saw eclipses as propitious moments for divination and making important decisions. Kings could see them as signs of good or bad omens for their reign. Ceremonies were held not only to protect the sun, but also to interpret the messages of the gods and guide the future actions of rulers. These practices testify to the importance of astronomy and religion in Mayan culture, where every celestial phenomenon was a sacred dialogue between men and the divine powers.

Fact 72 - Mayan pottery was used to store food

The Maya excelled in the art of pottery, creating vessels that were not only decorative but also highly functional for food storage. These potteries, often made from local clay, were carefully shaped and fired to ensure durability. The vessels came in a variety of shapes and sizes, suitable for storing different types of food such as corn, beans and chillies, which were essential components of their diet.

Pottery was often decorated with symbolic motifs and vivid paintings depicting scenes of daily life or protective deities. These decorations were not only aesthetic; they also carried ritual and practical meanings. For example, jars used to store corn might be decorated with symbols associated with fertility and prosperity, reinforcing the idea that the gods were watching over the food supply.

Food storage was crucial in Mayan societies, especially in times of drought or scarcity. The Maya used hermetically sealed pottery to protect food from parasites and humidity, preserving their food for extended periods. Some pottery was even designed with special lids or closures to ensure better preservation. This demonstrated an advanced understanding of storage needs and the ability to extend the shelf life of foodstuffs.

In addition to their domestic use, pottery was also used for trade, transporting food over long distances. Maya merchants filled them with precious goods such as cocoa or honey, transporting resources between cities. Jars and pots, often marked with distinctive motifs, made it easy to identify the origins of products and merchants, much like modern brand names.

The importance of pottery in Mayan culture was also reflected in its use in funeral rites. The Maya placed pots filled with food in graves to accompany the deceased into the afterlife. These objects served as a link between the living and the dead, ensuring that ancestors never ran out of food in the spirit world. Thus, pottery was not limited to a simple utilitarian function; it also embodied profound spiritual values, demonstrating the importance of continuity and preservation in Mayan culture.

Fact 73 - Mayan temples honored specific gods

The majestic and imposing Mayan temples were not simply impressive architectural structures; they served above all to honor specific deities from the Mayan pantheon. Each temple was dedicated to a particular god, reflecting the needs and beliefs of the community that erected it. For example, the Temple of the Great Jaguar at Tikal was dedicated to the divinity of the sun and symbolized power and royalty.

These temples were often built at great heights, to bring the faithful closer to the gods and allow the priests to perform rituals visible to the whole community. The steep staircases leading to the top were not only physically challenging; they also represented an ascent to the divine. Each step was a reminder of the spiritual progression and respect due to the deities. Ceremonies conducted from these heights included offerings, sacrifices and prayers designed to appease or thank the gods.

Temple decoration was carefully chosen to reflect the appearance and attributes of the god being honored. Sculptures, frescoes and even architectural alignments responded to precise symbolisms. For example, the god of rain, Chaac, was often associated with water motifs and representations of snakes, omnipresent elements in the temples dedicated to him. The walls decorated with these symbols were a constant reminder to the Maya of the presence and importance of this divinity in their daily lives.

Each Maya city had its own emblematic temples, often dedicated to gods who represented the natural forces crucial to the community's survival, such as rain, sun and fertility. The temples of Chichen Itza, for example, included structures dedicated to Kukulkan, the feathered serpent, whose cult was central to the region. The play of light and shadow on the temples, such as the famous serpent effect of the Kukulkan temple during the equinoxes, further reinforced the idea that the gods were present and active in the human world.

Temples were not only places of worship, but also centers of knowledge and astronomical observation. They played a key role in planning rituals and agricultural calendars, based on celestial cycles. The priests, trained in these places, observed the movements of the stars to determine the propitious times for ceremonies and community actions. In this way, Mayan temples not only honored the gods; they also organized and guided the spiritual, social and economic life of the Mayan civilization, demonstrating the extent to which the divine permeated every aspect of their existence.

Fact 74 - The stars were considered sacred guides

For the Maya, the night sky was not just a starry canvas, but a sacred book filled with divine signs. The stars were seen as spiritual guides, lighting the way for important decisions and influencing earthly actions. By carefully observing the constellations, the Maya found answers to the mysteries of life and the cosmos. They saw these celestial bodies as spirits watching over them, interpreting the positions and movements of the stars as messages from the gods.

Priest-astronomers were in charge of deciphering these celestial messages. Thanks to their knowledge, they were able to predict crucial events such as eclipses or seasonal changes. These predictions were essential not only for agriculture, but also for rituals and warfare. Stellar alignments, such as those of the star Sirius or the constellation Pleiades, marked moments of spiritual renewal or celebration. The Maya believed that these alignments determined propitious times for planting, harvesting or fighting battles.

Maya buildings, particularly observatories and temples, were often oriented according to the stars. For example, the observatory at Chichen Itza, known as "El Caracol", was specifically designed to follow the movements of Venus, a star of great importance to the Mayans. The precision of their observations was such that they were able to track stellar cycles with remarkable accuracy, surpassing even other civilizations of their time.

Stars weren't just points of light in the sky for the Maya; they also represented divine beings and ancestors. Each star or group of stars could be associated with a god or mythical hero, adding a narrative and religious dimension to their observations. For example, the Maya associated the Pleiades constellation with a myth of renewal and fertility, a narrative that was reflected in seasonal festivals and agricultural practices.

As sacred guides, the stars were an integral part of Mayan daily life. They were consulted for decisions ranging from agricultural plantations to royal coronations. This connection to the stars testified to a profound link between the terrestrial world and the cosmos, a link that the Maya cultivated with meticulous attention and constant reverence. This intimate relationship with the stars underlines the ingenuity and spirituality of the Maya, who saw the night sky as a reflection of the divine and a celestial map of their destiny on Earth.

Fact 75 - Clay figurines tell ancient myths

The Maya used clay figurines to immortalize and transmit their mythological tales. These small sculptures, often found in graves and sacred places, depicted gods, heroes or mythical scenes, illustrating the beliefs and stories that structured their worldview. Each figurine, with its distinctive features and meticulous detail, recounted a part of the myths that formed the core of Mayan culture, acting as tangible supports for their rich oral tradition.

These figurines served a variety of purposes, from ritual offerings to objects of personal devotion. For example, some figurines depicted the rain god, Chaac, with his characteristic attributes such as the long trunk and droplet patterns, symbolizing his crucial role in agriculture. Peasants used them to invoke rain in times of drought, while other representations evoked specific episodes from Mayan mythology, such as the creation of the world or the exploits of the twin heroes of the Popol Vuh.

Workshops for the production of these figurines were numerous and often located near major ceremonial centers. Craftsmen molded clay with great skill, incorporating intricate details that made each piece unique. Figurines could be painted with natural pigments to accentuate certain aspects, such as the clothing of the gods or the specific attributes of each mythical character. Vivid colors and meticulous patterns added a living dimension to the stories depicted, transforming each figurine into a fragment of history frozen in time.

Archaeological excavations have revealed hundreds of these figurines in a variety of contexts, indicating their importance in Maya daily and religious life. In some cities, clay figurines were an integral part of funeral rites, placed in tombs to accompany the deceased into the afterlife. They often represented divine protectors or ancestors, reminding us that even after death, myths continued to guide and protect souls.

These clay figurines not only represented the deities, but also included everyday characters such as dancers, warriors and weavers. They reflected the many facets of Mayan society, linking the stories of the gods to the lives of mortals. By preserving these ancient tales in tangible form, clay figurines played a crucial role in the transmission of myths from generation to generation, keeping Mayan traditions and beliefs alive through the ages.

Fact 76 - Mayan calendars were carved in stone

The Maya engraved their calendars in stone, a practice that reflects the primordial importance they attached to time and its organization. These calendars were not simply tools for keeping track of the days; they were deeply rooted in religion, agriculture and daily life. Stelae and engraved monuments found in cities such as Tikal and Copán demonstrate the complexity of Mayan calendar systems, including the Tzolk'in, a 260-day ritual calendar, and the Haab', a 365-day solar calendar.

Each engraving on these stones was a meticulous work of art. The Maya used stone tools to carve intricate glyphs representing important dates and events. The engravings often included depictions of gods, kings or ceremonial scenes, making each calendar not only a tool for measuring time, but also an illustration of Mayan beliefs and rituals. These stones served as historical markers, recounting eclipses, Venus cycles and other celestial phenomena that the Maya observed with great precision.

One of the most famous of these engravings is that of the Quiriguá Turtle Monument, dating from 775 AD and showing a complex countdown of days inscribed in stone. These inscriptions were also used to celebrate the reigns of kings and commemorate important events such as coronations and military victories. Calendrical engravings were often erected in strategic locations in cities, such as central squares and temple entrances, where they could be seen and consulted by the population.

Calendars carved in stone demonstrated the Maya's mastery of astronomy and mathematics. By engraving these calendars, the Maya sought to understand and influence the course of time, linking celestial cycles to life on Earth. This connection between heaven and earth was essential to their worldview, and stone calendars were a tangible manifestation of this, enabling them to predict the seasons, plan harvests and organize religious rituals.

Looking at the stone calendars, you can still feel the importance of time in Mayan culture. These stones, carved centuries ago, continue to tell the story of the Maya's complex relationship with the cosmos. They show how, through stone, the Maya sought to impose an order on a universe perceived as in perpetual change, an order that guided every aspect of their existence. These calendars, remarkably accurate for their time, bear witness to the genius of the Maya and their relentless quest to understand and master the world around them.

Fact 77 - Jewelry was used to indicate Mayan social rank

Among the Maya, jewelry was more than just an ornament; it played a crucial role in society, indicating a person's social rank and status. The materials used for these adornments varied according to social position. Nobles and kings wore jewelry made of jade, gold or obsidian, symbols of wealth and power. Jade, in particular, was highly prized and often reserved for the elite, as it represented immortality and connection to the gods.

Engravings on stelae and frescoes frequently show kings and queens adorned with richly decorated necklaces, bracelets and crowns. In the Palenque ruins, for example, depictions of Pakal the Great show an ostentatious use of jewelry, ranging from large necklaces of jade beads to imposing earrings. These ornaments served to display not only personal wealth, but also the ruler's sacred link with the divine, thus reinforcing his authority over the people.

Priests and other religious figures also wore specific jewelry, often associated with their roles in rituals and ceremonies. Their finery included pendants representing sacred symbols or gods, designed to evoke spiritual power. Such jewelry served to distinguish their sacred role and mark their special connection with celestial forces, essential elements in conducting rites and sacrifices.

By contrast, the lower social classes, such as farmers and craftsmen, wore jewelry made of bone, wood or shells. Although these materials were less precious, they were no less symbolic, often carved with motifs that reflected personal or family beliefs. Maya jewelry, however simple, always had a meaning beyond its material value, helping to define identity and one's place in society.

The importance of jewelry in Mayan culture was also evident in funeral rites. The burials of the elite were often accompanied by rich finery, a reflection of their rank even in the afterlife. For example, the tomb of the Red Queen at Palenque contained not only human remains, but also an impressive array of jade and gold jewelry. This illustrates the Maya's belief in the need to preserve status symbols, even after death, and testifies to the continuity of rank and prestige beyond earthly life.

Fact 78 - Obelisks commemorate significant events

Obelisks, also called stelae by archaeologists, were central to Mayan culture, serving as monuments to commemorate significant events. These sculpted stone pillars were erected to celebrate military victories, alliances, ascensions to power and other crucial moments in Mayan history. Each obelisk was meticulously engraved with glyphs recounting the glorious tales of kings and nobles, transforming stone into an enduring archive of civilization's deeds.

One of the most famous stelae is found at Copán, depicting King 18-Rabbit in a richly ornamented garb, with inscriptions recounting his conquests and achievements. These monuments were not only tokens of power, but also political tools. They reminded everyone of the greatness and legitimacy of rulers, consolidating their authority with the people. Obelisks were often placed in the ceremonial centers of cities, visible to all and a fundamental element of the urban landscape.

The inscriptions engraved on the obelisks didn't just relate Facts; they included precise dates, inscribed according to the complex Mayan calendar system. This made it possible to situate each event in time with remarkable precision. This practice testified to the importance attached to chronology and historical recording, essential aspects of Mayan culture. By reading the glyphs, scribes were able to retrace the dynastic history and key moments of their civilization.

Obelisks were not limited to the stories of kings; they were also used to immortalize cosmic and religious events. For example, some Quiriguá monuments depict scenes of kings interacting with deities or mythical animals, illustrating the connection between earthly power and divine order. The Maya firmly believed in the intercession of the gods in human affairs, and obelisks were a reminder of this sacred connection.

Archaeological digs continue to reveal new stelae, adding new pieces to the complex puzzle of Mayan history. Each discovery brings new information about the battles, celebrations and even natural disasters that marked the various cities. Thus, obelisks, far more than mere blocks of stone, are the silent guardians of the Maya's collective memory, timeless witnesses to the triumphs and trials that shaped one of the most fascinating civilizations in human history.

Fact 79 - Shell instruments were used for ritual purposes

The Maya used shell instruments, notably conches, for their religious rituals and ceremonies. These instruments produced deep, powerful sounds, capable of reverberating through temples and public squares, marking the importance of the event. Conches were often decorated with intricate carvings depicting gods or sacred symbols, underlining their sacred role in communicating with deities.

During ceremonies, priests played the conch shell to summon the spirits or to announce the start of important rites. The sound of the conch, reminiscent of the sea, was perceived as a direct link with the aquatic gods and natural forces. For example, during rituals dedicated to the rain god Chaac, conch sounds could be interpreted as calls for rain, reinforcing the link between humans and the natural elements.

Conches were not only musical instruments; they were also used to mark specific moments in rituals, such as the offering of sacrifices or prayers. They often accompanied songs and dances, creating an atmosphere of sound that enveloped the participants and reinforced the spiritual impact of the ceremony. The bewitching sound of the conch symbolized divine authority and the call for unity between the earthly and spiritual worlds.

These shell instruments were also used in war ceremonies, to motivate warriors and intimidate the enemy. The sound of the conch, carried over long distances, was used to rally troops and give signals during battle. This use shows that conches played a strategic role beyond their ritual function, integrating music and sound into the most everyday and critical aspects of Mayan life.

Today, the use of conches in modern ceremonies recalls this ancient tradition, preserving a link with the Maya's spiritual past. They are still played at some contemporary festivities and rites, testifying to the persistence of ancestral practices and their continuing importance in the culture of Mayan descendants. Conches remain a powerful symbol of the connection between man, nature and the divine, uniting past and present through the breath of a shell.

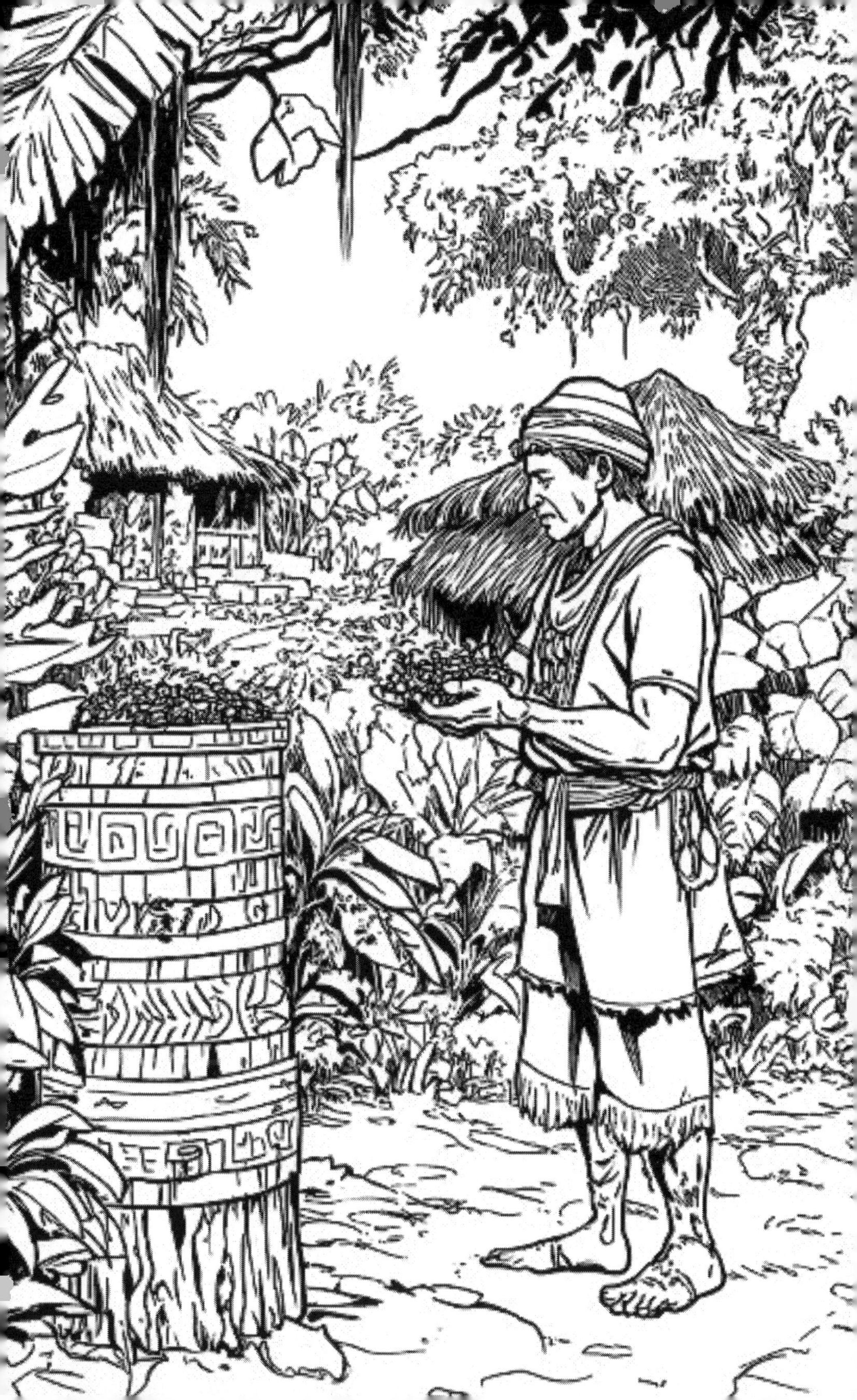

Fact 80 - The Mayans kept bees to harvest honey

The Maya were expert beekeepers, using stingless bees called Melipona beecheii to produce honey, a precious ingredient in their daily lives. Unlike the European bees we know today, these bees were domesticated in hollowed-out tree trunks called jobones or hobones, placed near houses and in gardens. The honey harvested was highly prized, not only as food, but also for its medicinal properties and its role in religious rituals.

Mayan honey was renowned for its unique flavor and different consistency, influenced by local flowers, such as those from balché trees and various tropical plants. This honey was not simply a sweetener; it was used in the preparation of fermented beverages such as balché, a ritual drink that played an important role in religious ceremonies and community celebrations. The link between beekeeping and spirituality was therefore very strong among the Maya.

The Maya saw bees not only as a source of honey, but also as sacred creatures, sent by the gods to bring their benefits to the land. Bee gods such as Ah Mucen Kab were worshipped in rituals designed to ensure the fertility of hives and the prosperity of beekeeping. These ceremonies included offerings of flowers, honey and sometimes even sacrifices to appease and honor the bees' protective spirits.

Mayan beekeeping was also a reflection of their deep understanding of nature and the environment. The Mayans knew how to maintain their hives, protect bees from predators, and maximize honey production without depleting natural resources. This sustainable management of beekeeping was part of a broader vision of the balance between man and nature, essential to their way of life. Bees were not only honey producers, but also crucial pollinators for agricultural crops.

Today, traces of this beekeeping tradition live on in certain Yucatán communities, where the Melipona bee continues to be bred, perpetuating an ancient know-how that goes back thousands of years. The honey produced by these bees remains a sought-after product, not only for its gustatory qualities, but also for its cultural heritage and its importance in traditional medicine. The techniques and beliefs surrounding Mayan beekeeping bear witness to the ingenuity and deep respect this civilization had for nature and its cycles.

Fact 81 - Mayan rituals invoked rain for crops

The Maya, who depended on agriculture for their livelihood, placed great importance on rituals invoking the rain, essential for successful harvests. The god of rain, Chaac, was at the heart of these practices. Ceremonies dedicated to Chaac often took place near cenotes or caves, places considered to be gateways to the underworld and the abodes of the gods. These rituals were intended to solicit abundant rainfall, essential for watering fields of corn, beans and squash.

During rain rituals, priests would make sacrifices and offerings, such as incense, food or even precious objects, to appease and satisfy Chaac. Sometimes, dances and songs accompanied by skin drums and conches were performed to attract the attention of the gods. The resonant sounds of these instruments were supposed to imitate thunder and lightning, symbolizing a direct appeal to the forces of nature to bring the water necessary for life.

Ceremonies invoking rain were particularly intense during periods of drought. At such critical times, the Maya believed that divine intervention was the only way to save their crops. Prayers became more fervent, and sacrifices more substantial, as every drop of rain could determine the survival of communities. Prolonged drought could lead to famine, making these rituals all the more vital and meaningful.

Observing natural phenomena, such as cloud movements or animal behavior, was an integral part of rituals. The Maya interpreted these signs as answers from the gods to their prayers. The priests, experts in reading omens, adapted rituals to these observations to maximize their chances of success. This shows the extent to which rituals were not only religious, but also closely linked to a profound understanding of nature and its cycles.

These practices continue to this day in some communities descended from the Maya, where rain rituals are still observed. Although they have evolved, these rituals continue to reflect the Maya's deep respect and dependence on natural forces, testifying to a culture that saw the earth and sky as essential partners in the cycle of agricultural life. These traditions are a living legacy that links current generations to the ancient rituals of their ancestors.

Fact 82 - Animal sculptures represented Mayan gods

In Mayan civilization, animals held a central place not only in daily life, but also in religion. Animal sculptures were often more than mere artistic representations: they embodied the gods and spirits of the natural world. For example, the jaguar, feared and respected, was frequently carved to symbolize power and royalty, associated with deities such as the sun god and the god of war.

The Maya believed that certain animals possessed divine qualities or were manifestations of the gods themselves. Sculptures of feathered snakes, representing Kukulcán, embodied fertility and the sky. These ornate, imposing representations could be found on temple facades, stelae and even ritual objects, a constant reminder of the presence of the gods in Mayan life.

Mayan sculptors used a variety of materials to create these works: stone, jade and even obsidian. Each material was chosen for its symbolic properties and beauty, reinforcing the link between the earthly world and the divine. The meticulous detail and realism of these sculptures reflected not only the artistic talent of the Maya, but also their profound respect for the animal world and its links with their spiritual beliefs.

Animal sculptures also played an important role in rituals and ceremonies. Turtle effigies, for example, symbolized the earth and creation, and were used in rituals related to fertility and prosperity. These sculptures served as tangible bridges between humans and the gods, facilitating communication with divine forces through offerings and prayers.

Archaeological sites abound with these sculptures, each telling a unique story about Mayan beliefs and religious practices. Through these works, we discover a civilization that saw each creature as a divine messenger, capable of influencing human events through its connection with the gods. Maya animal sculptures continue to amaze with their complexity and symbolic depth, reminding us that for the Maya, the natural and spiritual worlds were inextricably linked.

Fact 83 - Tapestries adorned Mayan royal palaces

In Mayan royal palaces, tapestries played an essential role not only as decoration, but also as symbols of power and prestige. These textile works, rich in color and intricate patterns, were carefully woven by skilled craftsmen, often using precious materials such as cotton and maguey fibers. The motifs depicted mythological scenes, royal exploits or religious symbols, linking kings to gods and ancestors.

Tapestries were also used to demonstrate the wealth and influence of sovereigns. In the throne rooms and private chambers of palaces, they covered walls, thrones and even altars, creating an atmosphere of grandeur and divinity. They were not simply decorative objects, but elements that reinforced the authority and legitimacy of rulers, reminding all visitors of the power of royalty.

The art of tapestry weaving was often passed down from generation to generation, and each piece could take months or even years to complete. Designs varied according to region and time, but all shared a deep sense of detail and symmetry, characteristic of Mayan art. Vivid colors, obtained from natural dyes such as indigo and cochineal red, added a captivating visual dimension, enhancing the splendor of the palaces.

Tapestries were not only admired for their aesthetics, they were also imbued with profound meanings. For example, a tapestry depicting the corn god could symbolize abundance and prosperity for the coming reign. These textile works were therefore powerful tools for expressing the aspirations and values of Mayan royalty, blending art and symbolism inseparably.

Today, the rare fragments found by archaeologists offer a valuable insight into life in Mayan palaces. They bear witness to the extraordinary skill of Maya weavers and the importance accorded to textile art in Maya culture. Far more than mere ornaments, these tapestries were statements of power, faith and tradition, capturing the essence of Mayan civilization in every thread and motif.

Fact 84 - The Maya celebrated harvests with special festivals

The Maya attached great importance to agricultural cycles, and harvests were key moments in their calendar. To mark these events, they organized special feasts dedicated to the gods of fertility and the earth. These celebrations, often centered around corn, a sacred and essential food for the Maya, were intended to thank the deities for their generosity and to ensure prosperous future harvests.

Harvest festivals were rich in ritual and ceremony. They included food offerings, ritual dances and prayers. Priests played a central role, leading communities in rites to honor gods such as Yum Kaax, the god of corn, and Chac, the god of rain. These moments strengthened the bond between the Maya and their deities, while solidifying social cohesion within the cities.

During these festivities, banquets were organized, bringing families together around dishes prepared with the products of the harvest. Corn, in the form of tamales or fermented beverages such as balché, was at the heart of the meals. These feasts not only served to feed, but also to symbolize the abundance and prosperity that the gods had bestowed. It was a time for sharing and collective celebration.

Dance and song often accompanied these celebrations. The Mayas dressed in their finest garments, sometimes adorned with feathers and jade jewelry, to dance in circles around altars or central plazas. Musicians, playing instruments made of wood, bone or shell, gave rhythm to these festive moments, creating an atmosphere that was both joyous and sacred. Every movement and note was imbued with spiritual significance, linking participants to the cycles of nature.

Harvest festivals were also an opportunity for rulers to show their generosity and connection with the gods. Games and competitions could be organized, showcasing the agility and strength of participants, while rulers offered gifts to their subjects to mark the occasion. Thus, these harvest celebrations were much more than mere festivities: they were a reflection of the social and cosmic order, a communion between the Maya, their land and their deities.

Fact 85 - Bone flutes used to accompany religious rituals

The Maya used bone flutes in their religious rituals, integrating music into their spiritual practices. These flutes, made from the bones of animals such as deer and birds, produced deep, melodious sounds that resonated in temples and sacred places. Each flute was often adorned with symbolic engravings or motifs representing deities, accentuating their sacred role and connection to the gods.

The music played on these flutes not only served to create a mystical atmosphere; it also had a functional role in rituals. The sounds of the flute guided the movements of priests and participants, marking the stages of ceremonies. Whether invocations, sacrifices or celebrations of natural cycles, bone flutes provided an essential aural dimension, linking people to spirits through the vibration of sound.

Flutes often accompanied sacred dances, performances that mimicked mythological stories or the exploits of the gods. Elaborately costumed priests and dancers would follow the rhythm of the flutes, creating a symbiosis between music and movement. This dialogue between sound and body was seen as a form of direct communication with celestial entities, making prayers and offerings more powerful.

Major ceremonies, such as solstices or eclipses, were privileged moments for the use of these instruments. At these events, the sounds of bone flutes mingled with those of other instruments such as drums and conches, forming a symphony dedicated to the gods. The low, piercing tones of the flutes were said to imitate the voices of spirits and ancestors, adding a layer of meaning to each note played.

Bone flutes also testify to the musical and artisanal skills of the Maya. The precision required to carve these instruments and adjust their tones shows a thorough knowledge of acoustics and materials. In playing the flute, the Maya did more than simply produce music; they invoked a sacred tradition, linking each breath of air to the mysticism of their culture, marking religious rites with their unique sonic imprint.

Fact 86 - Rituals honored ancestors and spirits

The Maya practiced complex rituals to honor their ancestors and spirits, integrating these ceremonies into their daily lives and spirituality. Ancestors occupied a central place in Mayan culture, regarded as invisible protectors and guides. By celebrating their memory, the Maya sought to strengthen the links between the world of the living and that of the spirits, thus ensuring the harmony and protection of their community.

Rites in honor of the ancestors included offerings of food, drink and symbolic objects. These offerings were placed in domestic altars or in sacred places such as caves, considered to be passageways to the afterlife. The Maya believed that ancestral spirits could influence harvests, health and prosperity, hence the importance of honoring them regularly to maintain their favor.

Ceremonies also involved invocations and prayers to the spirits of nature, who were seen as living entities intervening in people's daily lives. Priests played a crucial role, acting as intermediaries between humans and supernatural forces. With their songs and the use of sacred instruments such as flutes and drums, they created an atmosphere conducive to spiritual communication, seeking to attract the benevolence of the spirits.

During these rituals, masks representing ancestors or spirits were often worn by the participants. These masks, made of ceramic or wood, symbolized the presence of the ancestors among the living and their active participation in the ceremonies. By wearing these masks, the Maya were not merely recalling the past; they were literally incarnating their ancestors, allowing these revered figures to live through them and participate in community life.

Rituals of homage to ancestors and spirits were an integral part of major Mayan celebrations, such as end-of-cycle ceremonies and harvest festivals. They served to strengthen social ties by uniting community members around a common cause: honoring those who had gone before them and asking for protection from the invisible forces that governed their world. These ritual practices, deeply rooted in Mayan culture, bear witness to the complex, interconnected vision they had of the world, where each ritual gesture carried multiple, sacred meanings.

Fact 87 - Carved stones recount military exploits

The Maya used carved stones to immortalize their military exploits, turning each victory into a story engraved in stone. These carvings, often found on stelae and monuments, were used to commemorate conquests and celebrate the power of kings and warriors. Each carving was carefully designed to tell a story, from the preparation of battles to the capture of enemies, offering a visual testimony to the bravery and military strategies of the Maya.

Steles were the preferred medium for these sculpted narratives. Erected in the central squares of cities, they were visible to all and were a powerful means of propaganda. Meticulous details of war dress, weapons and captured prisoners were depicted with great precision. These images were accompanied by glyphs that specified the names of kings, the dates of battles and the results obtained, thus providing a detailed chronology of military events.

These carvings not only depicted battles, but also served to legitimize the rulers' power. By engraving their exploits on stone, Maya kings reinforced their position and recalled their divine right to rule. The scenes often showed the king triumphant, dominating his enemies, symbolizing not only military victory but also spiritual superiority. Engraved exploits were thus a political tool, consolidating the sovereign's authority and reputation among his people and rivals.

Carved stones also offered a means of passing on stories from one generation to the next. They represented a tangible link with the past, where each carving became a chapter in the collective story. For example, engravings found at Copán and Tikal depict famous battles and strategic alliances, enabling archaeologists to reconstruct complex narratives of wars and rivalries between cities. The images and glyphs reveal not only the details of the battles but also the motives behind these wars, whether economic, territorial or religious.

The Maya also used these stones to celebrate major victories that redefined alliances and balances of power in the region. When a city won a significant victory, stelae were erected to proclaim the triumph to all who passed by. These monuments were often accompanied by grandiose ceremonies, including offerings and dances, further reinforcing the impact of these engraved narratives.

Fact 88 - Bows and arrows were used for hunting and rituals

The Maya used bows and arrows not only for hunting, but also for ceremonial purposes. These weapons, essential for daily survival, played a crucial role in hunting animals such as deer, birds and monkeys, providing a vital source of food and materials for tools and clothing. Their mastery of bows and arrows testified to their skill and knowledge of the terrain, making every hunt both a challenge and a necessity.

Apart from their practical use, bows and arrows also had an important symbolic dimension in Mayan rites. They were often used in ceremonies to honor the gods of hunting and war. These rituals sometimes included hunting simulations, where bows and arrows were used to show respect for animal spirits and to ensure abundant catches. Arrows could be adorned with colorful feathers and sacred motifs, transforming a simple tool into a ritual object.

Bows and arrows were also part of rites of passage and victory celebrations. During certain ceremonies, young warriors demonstrated their archery skills as a rite of initiation, symbolizing their passage to adulthood and entry into the community of hunters or warriors. These demonstrations were accompanied by song and dance, creating a spectacle that left a lasting impression and strengthened social bonds.

In Mayan mythological accounts, bows and arrows frequently appear as symbols of protection and power. They are often associated with legendary gods and heroes who used these weapons to defeat enemies or supernatural forces. These tales served to teach the values of courage, cunning and respect for nature, while underlining the importance of bows and arrows in Mayan culture.

Arrows were sometimes used in rituals to invoke natural forces, such as rain or the fertility of the land. By shooting arrows into the sky or in symbolic directions, priests hoped to influence the elements and ensure prosperous harvests. These rituals combined both practical skills and spiritual beliefs, demonstrating the extent to which bows and arrows were integrated into Mayan daily and religious life.

Fact 89 - Offerings to the rain gods were frequent

The Maya attached great importance to the rain gods, particularly Chaac, the god of rain and water. In a region where survival depended heavily on climatic conditions, offerings to the rain gods were essential to ensure abundant harvests and fertile land. The Maya believed that the rains were a direct result of the gods' moods, so it was crucial to maintain their favor through regular rituals.

These offerings often took the form of symbolic sacrifices, such as fruits, flowers and incense, deposited in cenotes, natural wells regarded as gateways to the world of the gods. The cenotes were seen as sacred places where the Maya came into direct contact with Chaac. Archaeologists have discovered precious objects, such as jade jewelry and pottery, thrown into these wells during rituals to appease the water deities.

Rituals involving offerings could be elaborate and dramatic, sometimes involving animal sacrifices or even, on rare and particularly important occasions, human sacrifices. These ceremonies were conducted by priests, who invoked the gods through song, dance and prayer. Every element of the ritual was meticulously orchestrated to ensure its effectiveness and to convey to the gods the Maya's desperate need for water.

Ceremonies often took place during periods of drought, when water became a critical resource. The Maya, dependent on harvests of corn, beans and squash, saw rain not only as an agricultural blessing, but also as proof of divine approval. The slightest delay in the rains could provoke fear and uncertainty, prompting communities to multiply offerings in an attempt to restore the balance.

These ritual practices demonstrate the depth of the connection between the Maya and their natural environment. For them, the gods were living entities, present in every drop of rain, every source of water. Offerings to the rain gods were not just acts of religious devotion, but an integral part of their way of life, a sacred exchange designed to ensure the survival of their people and their culture.

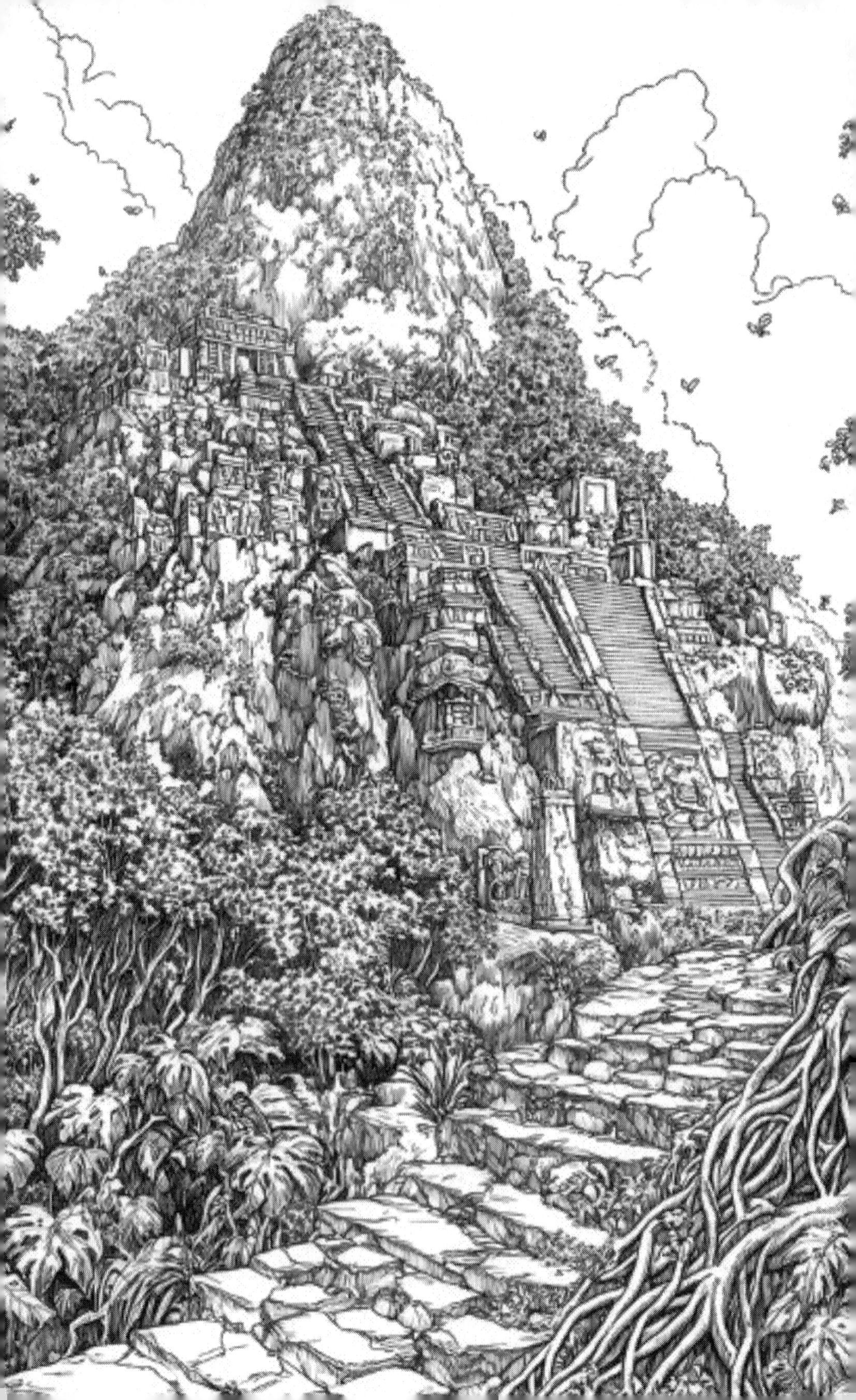

Fact 90 - Mountains were seen as sacred places

For the Maya, mountains were more than just geological formations. They were seen as symbols of divinity and the connection between the earthly world and the heavens. Because of their height and majesty, mountains were considered privileged meeting points with the gods. They embodied the abode of spirits and divinities, notably those associated with rain, fertility and land protection.

The mountains also played a central role in Mayan rituals. Priests held ceremonies there to honor the gods and solicit their benevolence. These rituals included offerings of jade, feathers and sometimes blood, considered necessary sacrifices to maintain the balance between the human and divine worlds. By climbing mountains to perform these rituals, the Maya sought to draw closer to their gods, both physically and spiritually.

Some mountains were particularly revered and even associated with specific gods. For example, in some regions, mountains were dedicated to Chaac, the god of rain, reflecting the importance of precipitation for agricultural crops. Mountains were home to caves and natural cavities, which were also seen as passages to the subterranean and celestial worlds. These places were carefully chosen for important rituals, reinforcing their sacred status.

Mayan mythological narratives abound with references to mountains as pillars of creation and refuges for ancestors. They were often evoked in stories of legendary heroes and mythical battles, underlining their central role in the Mayan imagination. These mountains represented not only strength and stability, but also the challenges and spiritual trials that believers had to overcome to achieve wisdom and harmony.

The sacredness of mountains was also reflected in Mayan architecture, where pyramids and temples were built to imitate their form. In erecting these structures, the Maya sought to reproduce the grandeur and spirituality of the mountains on earth, transforming their cities into microcosms of the divine cosmos. Mountains, in all their majesty and mystery, continued to inspire and guide Mayan spiritual practices, linking the daily lives of men to the eternal realms of the gods.

Fact 91 - Rituals for lunar eclipses were mysterious

The Maya saw lunar eclipses as events of great cosmic importance, often imbued with mystery and awe. For them, an eclipse was not just an astronomical phenomenon, but a sign from the gods, sometimes interpreted as an omen of upheaval or bad omens. Lunar eclipses, in particular, were associated with celestial battles between the forces of good and evil, symbolized by the moon and the mythological creatures seeking to devour it.

To appease the dark forces and protect their world, the Maya performed complex rituals during lunar eclipses. These rituals included offerings of food, incense and sometimes even animal sacrifices to attract the gods' benevolence. Mayan priests, guardians of sacred knowledge, played a central role in these ceremonies, reciting specific songs and prayers to invoke divine powers capable of restoring cosmic order. The rituals were often accompanied by symbolic dances and the use of instruments such as drums and conches to punctuate the invocations.

Lunar eclipses were also seen as propitious moments for divination. Priests interpreted the progress of the eclipse and celestial signs to predict future events, such as harvests, wars or political success. These readings of the sky were shared with rulers and the community, reinforcing the priests' position as essential intermediaries between the world of men and that of the gods. Predictions based on lunar eclipses often influenced the political decisions and military strategies of Mayan rulers.

Rituals linked to lunar eclipses usually took place on platforms or in temples specially dedicated to observing the sky. These structures were built with a particular orientation to follow the movements of the moon and stars, reflecting the importance attached to astronomy in Mayan culture. The community's participation in these rituals created a collective bond, a kind of communion with celestial forces, where each individual contributed to the effort to maintain cosmic balance.

Despite their mystery, lunar eclipse rituals demonstrate the Maya's obsession with understanding and influencing the cycles of the universe. These ceremonies reveal a deep connection between the Maya people and celestial phenomena, a relationship marked by reverence, awe and a constant desire to maintain harmony between the earth and the cosmos. For the Maya, lunar eclipses were doorways to an invisible world, where mortals could glimpse the designs of the gods and attempt to influence them through their devotions and sacrifices.

Fact 92 - Jade masks were worn for funerals

Jade masks were precious and sacred artifacts for the Maya, often associated with the funeral rituals of elites and rulers. These masks, made from carefully carved pieces of jade, embodied not only wealth and power, but also deep spiritual significance. At funerals, jade masks were placed over the face of the deceased, symbolizing the soul's transition to the afterlife and ensuring divine protection during this journey.

Making jade masks required exceptional skill. Artisans selected pieces of the purest jade, often green in color, the Mayan symbol of life and regeneration. Each piece of jade was meticulously cut and polished, then assembled to form the mask. Facial features, such as the eyes and mouth, were depicted in a stylized manner, reflecting both the individual features of the deceased and the aesthetic ideals of Mayan society.

These funerary masks were not just objects of prestige; they played a crucial role in Mayan beliefs about death and immortality. The Maya believed that jade possessed magical properties capable of conferring immortality. Thus, by covering the faces of the deceased with these masks, they hoped not only to honor the dead, but also to guarantee their safe and glorious passage into the afterlife. The jade mask served as an eternal face, preserving the essence and identity of the deceased for all eternity.

Jade masks were often found in the tombs of kings and nobles, underlining their high status and connection with the gods. For example, the discovery of the jade mask of K'inich Janaab' Pakal, one of Palenque's greatest rulers, illustrates the importance of these objects. This mask, composed of several hundred pieces of finely-worked jade, reflected not only the high level of Maya craftsmanship, but also their complex vision of life after death.

Jade masks thus represent a unique fusion of art, spirituality and political power in Mayan culture. They bear witness to the way in which the Maya honored their dead and sought to protect them in the afterlife. By wearing these masks at burial, the Maya hoped that their ancestors would continue to watch over them, ensuring the prosperity and continuity of their lineage.

Fact 93 - Rituals protected harvests from disasters

The Maya attached great importance to protecting their crops, as agriculture was central to their survival and prosperity. To avoid natural disasters such as drought, storms or pest infestations, they organized specific rituals designed to appease the gods and invoke their protection over the fields. These rituals included prayers, songs and offerings, often performed in sacred places such as caves or mountains, where they believed the spirits of the gods resided.

One of the gods most often invoked in these rituals was Chaac, the god of rain. The Maya offered him sacrifices of food, cocoa and even animals, in the hope of obtaining abundant and regular rainfall, essential for the growth of maize, their main crop. In some regions, rituals even involved human sacrifice to appease the gods during periods of severe drought, demonstrating the crucial importance of these practices to their survival.

Ceremonies could also include ritual dances and music, using traditional instruments such as drums and bone flutes, to attract the attention of the deities. Every movement, every note played had a precise meaning and was part of a symbolic dialogue with supernatural forces. The priests, central figures in these rituals, dressed in elaborate costumes, often adorned with feathers and jewels, to symbolically approach the gods they sought to invoke.

In addition to offerings, the Maya used astronomical calendars to determine the most auspicious times to hold these rituals. They carefully observed lunar cycles and star positions, believing that celestial movements could influence terrestrial events, including climatic conditions. This synchronization with natural cycles testified to their sophisticated understanding of the natural world and their ability to integrate this knowledge into their daily and spiritual lives.

These rituals demonstrate the extent to which the Maya saw their environment as an extension of the divine world. Natural disasters were not simply physical events, but imbalances between the world of men and that of the gods. Through their rituals, they sought to restore harmony and guarantee prosperous harvests, thus ensuring the continuity of their civilization.

Fact 94 - Botanical gardens had rare medicinal plants

The Mayans possessed an in-depth knowledge of plants and their medicinal properties, which they cultivated in specially laid-out botanical gardens. These gardens, located near urban centers or in temples, served as veritable natural pharmacies. They contained a wide variety of rare and precious plants, carefully selected for their therapeutic virtues. Herbs used to treat fevers, roots with anti-inflammatory properties, and leaves to treat infections were all part of this botanical heritage.

These gardens were not simply places of cultivation, but also sacred spaces where nature and the spiritual met. Plants were cultivated with extreme care, sometimes with specific rituals to guarantee their efficacy. Priests and healers, trained in the knowledge of plants, would come here to gather the ingredients needed for their potions and remedies, often integrating these substances into healing ceremonies or divinatory practices.

The use of medicinal plants went far beyond mere physical treatment. The Maya believed that certain plants possessed spiritual powers capable of purifying the spirit or protecting against evil spirits. For example, the copal plant, used to make incense, was burned for its soothing and purifying effects, both for the environment and the soul. This holistic approach to medicine reflected their worldview, in which body, mind and nature were deeply interconnected.

Archaeological discoveries have revealed the importance of these gardens in Mayan life. Traces of medicinal plants have been found in funerary contexts, indicating that they were also used to accompany the deceased into the afterlife. This shows the sacred value the Maya placed on these plants, not only for the living, but also for those who had passed on to the next world. These practices testify to the complexity and depth of their botanical knowledge.

The organization of Mayan botanical gardens illustrates their mastery of agriculture and the surrounding ecosystem. They selected species according to soil, water requirements and sunlight, demonstrating an advanced understanding of the interactions between plants and their environment. This meticulous management ensured not only the availability of necessary remedies, but also the preservation of biodiversity and natural resources, essential to their survival and prosperity.

Fact 95 - Mayan monuments were aligned with the stars

The Maya had a profound relationship with the sky, and this is reflected in the alignment of their monuments with the stars. They built their temples, pyramids and other edifices according to the celestial movements, in particular of the stars, sun and moon. This practice was not only architectural, but also symbolic and religious, aimed at harmonizing their constructions with the cycles of the cosmos. In this way, each monument became an astronomical observatory, a gateway to the universe.

One of the most striking examples is the site of Chichen Itza, where the imposing temple of Kukulcán is precisely aligned with the equinoxes. During these events, an optical illusion occurs, creating the appearance of a snake descending the temple stairs, representing the god Kukulcán, or feathered serpent. This architectural precision demonstrates their advanced knowledge of astronomy and their ability to incorporate this knowledge into their architecture.

This celestial alignment also served calendrical purposes. The Maya used their monuments to mark important events in their calendar, such as solstices and equinoxes. These key moments dictated the rhythm of their daily lives, governing agricultural seasons, religious rituals and even political decisions. Structures such as the E-Groups, specific architectural ensembles, were designed to follow the sunrise at different times of the year, demonstrating the importance of astronomy in time management.

Monuments aligned with the stars also enabled the Maya to connect with their gods, often associated with celestial bodies. The sun god, Kinich Ahau, and the moon were central deities in their pantheon, and their movements in the sky dictated essential aspects of Mayan life. So, by aligning their buildings with these stars, they were not only making an act of faith, they were literally inserting their world into the very fabric of the cosmos.

The alignment of monuments with the stars illustrates the sophistication of Mayan engineering and urban planning. They were not only builders of imposing structures, but also keen observers of the sky, able to translate their astronomical knowledge into lasting monuments. These alignments are no accident; they testify to the rigor and craftsmanship of a civilization that saw in each stone laid a relationship with the immensity of the universe, a reflection of their perpetual quest for harmony between the terrestrial and celestial worlds.

Fact 96 - Statues honored Mayan heroes and kings

The Maya erected statues to honor their heroes and kings, celebrating their exploits and importance in society. These statues, often carved in stone or stucco, were idealized representations of royal figures and famous warriors, designed to immortalize their glory and power. The statues not only reflected the physical appearance of these figures, but also their divine or semi-divine status, linking them directly to the gods and the cosmic order.

These statues generally stood in the central squares of cities or near temples, symbolizing the continuing presence and protection of the ancestors over the people. At Tikal, for example, stelae representing the kings were erected along the main squares, sometimes accompanied by sculptures of jaguars or eagles, symbols of power and royalty. Each statue was carefully carved to include hieroglyphic inscriptions recounting the great military victories, strategic alliances and sacred acts performed by the kings.

The art of carving these statues was highly elaborate, requiring in-depth knowledge of the stone and great precision. Mayan sculptors were highly respected artists, often commissioned by the nobility to create these works destined to last for centuries. Details of clothing, jewelry and royal attributes were meticulously reproduced, reinforcing the aura of majesty and authority of the figures depicted. Each element had a precise meaning, such as an elaborate headdress symbolizing connection with the divine world.

Statues also played a role in public rituals, serving as focal points for ceremonies. During important festivals or commemorations, they were often adorned with flowers, incense and sometimes even sacrifices. The Maya believed that these statues contained the spiritual essence of kings and heroes, transforming them into mediators between humans and the gods. As such, they were not just stone monuments, but living entities who continued to influence the destiny of the community.

This practice of commemorating with statues was part of a wider tradition of Mayan iconography, where art and religion were inextricably linked. By erecting statues to honor their heroes and kings, the Maya expressed their respect for the figures who had shaped their history and reinforced their own collective identity. These works, charged with symbolism and devotion, were pillars of Mayan culture, embodying the epic tales and values that animated them.

Fact 97 - The drums were made from unique natural materials

The Maya crafted drums using carefully selected natural materials, giving their instruments a special sound and importance in their rituals and celebrations. These drums were often made from hollowed wood, such as cedar or rosewood, chosen for its robustness and resonance. Animal skins, mainly those of deer or jaguar, were stretched over the body of the drum, each type of skin providing a distinct tonality.

Drum-making was an art in itself, requiring craftsmen to be highly precise and to understand the acoustic properties of the materials used. The craftsmen, respected for their skills, knew how to select the most suitable woods and mastered the techniques of preparing and treating the skins to obtain the desired sound. Drums varied in size, from small portable instruments to large ceremonial drums capable of producing deep, powerful sounds.

These drums were not only musical instruments, but also sacred objects used in rituals to invoke the gods or accompany ritual dances. During ceremonies, the beating of the drums created an atmosphere conducive to trance and communion with the spiritual world. For example, during rites dedicated to Chaac, the god of rain, the sound of drums resounded to call down beneficial rain, marking the union between heaven and earth.

Drums were sometimes decorated with engravings and symbolic motifs, often depicting totem animals or mythological scenes. These decorations added a visual dimension to the spiritual importance of the instrument, making it not only functional, but also aesthetically significant. A drum adorned with a feathered serpent, for example, recalled the presence of Kukulcán, the serpent god, and lent the instrument a particular power during rites.

The use of unique natural materials to make the drums illustrates the ingenuity of the Maya and their deep connection with nature. Each instrument, through its design and materials, told a story and carried within it the elements of the earth and animals. This enabled the Maya to strengthen their bond with the natural forces they worshipped, and to express their gratitude to the elements that made up their world.

Fact 98 - The Maya used glyphs to record laws

The Maya developed a complex writing system based on glyphs, used not only to tell stories and record important events, but also to record the laws and regulations of their societies. This system of glyphs, carved in stone, engraved on stelae or painted on codexes, was an essential tool for codifying and transmitting the rules that governed the daily life of Mayan city-states. Each glyph could represent a word, an idea or a sound, and their combination enabled precise expression of legal concepts.

Inscriptions of laws in glyphs were often placed on public monuments, such as steles or lintels, where they were visible to all members of the community. These inscriptions might detail laws concerning tribute, property rights, or obligations to rulers and gods. For example, a stela found at Piedras Negras features glyphs describing the duties of citizens towards the king, including specific contributions to be provided for religious ceremonies.

The use of glyphs to record laws reflected the importance of legality and social order in Mayan societies. Scribes, often from the nobility, played a crucial role as guardians of the written law. Their mastery of glyphs gave them significant power, as they were responsible for the preservation and dissemination of legal texts. These scribes could be called upon to document royal decisions or agreements between cities, thus serving as official witnesses and guarantors of justice.

The glyphs used for laws were sometimes accompanied by depictions of royal figures or gods, thus reinforcing the divine or royal authority of the texts. For example, bas-reliefs at Copán show kings holding batons of command, with glyphic inscriptions describing the laws they promulgated. This iconography underlined the link between earthly power and divine forces, reminding us that laws were not only human but also invested with a sacred character.

Thanks to their writing in glyphs, the Maya were also able to record legislative reforms or modifications, thus ensuring the continuity and adaptation of laws across generations. Codexes, although rare due to their destruction by the Spanish colonists, bear witness to this written tradition. These documents, produced on media such as fig bark paper, contained detailed information on rituals, calendars and laws, offering invaluable insight into how the Maya structured and managed their society.

Fact 99 - The Mayans air-conditioned their cities

The Mayans, living in stiflingly hot and often humid regions, developed ingenious systems to cool their cities and make living spaces more comfortable. Contrary to popular belief, they were not content to rely on the shade of trees and buildings. They implemented sophisticated solutions, such as the strategic orientation of buildings and the use of natural materials that favored air circulation and minimized heat accumulation.

One of the most remarkable techniques was the integration of natural ventilation systems into architectural structures. Temples and palaces were built with small openings and courtyards that allowed air to circulate freely, creating natural draughts. This helped maintain a cooler temperature inside, even on the hottest days. The Maya also used straw or palm-leaf roofs to insulate buildings and prevent heat build-up.

Reservoirs and bodies of water also played a key role in the cooling systems of Mayan cities. By integrating water basins near dwellings and public spaces, they created cooler microclimates through evaporation. These bodies of water were also used for irrigation and other domestic needs, demonstrating the extent to which the Maya knew how to make intelligent use of natural resources to improve their quality of life.

In some cities, the Maya built terraces and raised platforms that not only facilitated the flow of fresh air, but also provided protection against flooding. These terraces could be used for urban agriculture or community activities, while ensuring continuous natural ventilation. The design reflected both aesthetic and practical concerns, maximizing thermal comfort while enhancing the urban environment.

Finally, building orientations were carefully planned to take advantage of prevailing winds. Main entrances were often positioned to catch the breeze, and walls were built to provide shade during the hottest hours of the day. This attention to the orientation and layout of structures reflects Mayan ingenuity in managing climate and improving urban living conditions. These methods show that, long before modern advances, the Maya had a deep understanding of their environment and knew how to take advantage of it to meet their needs.

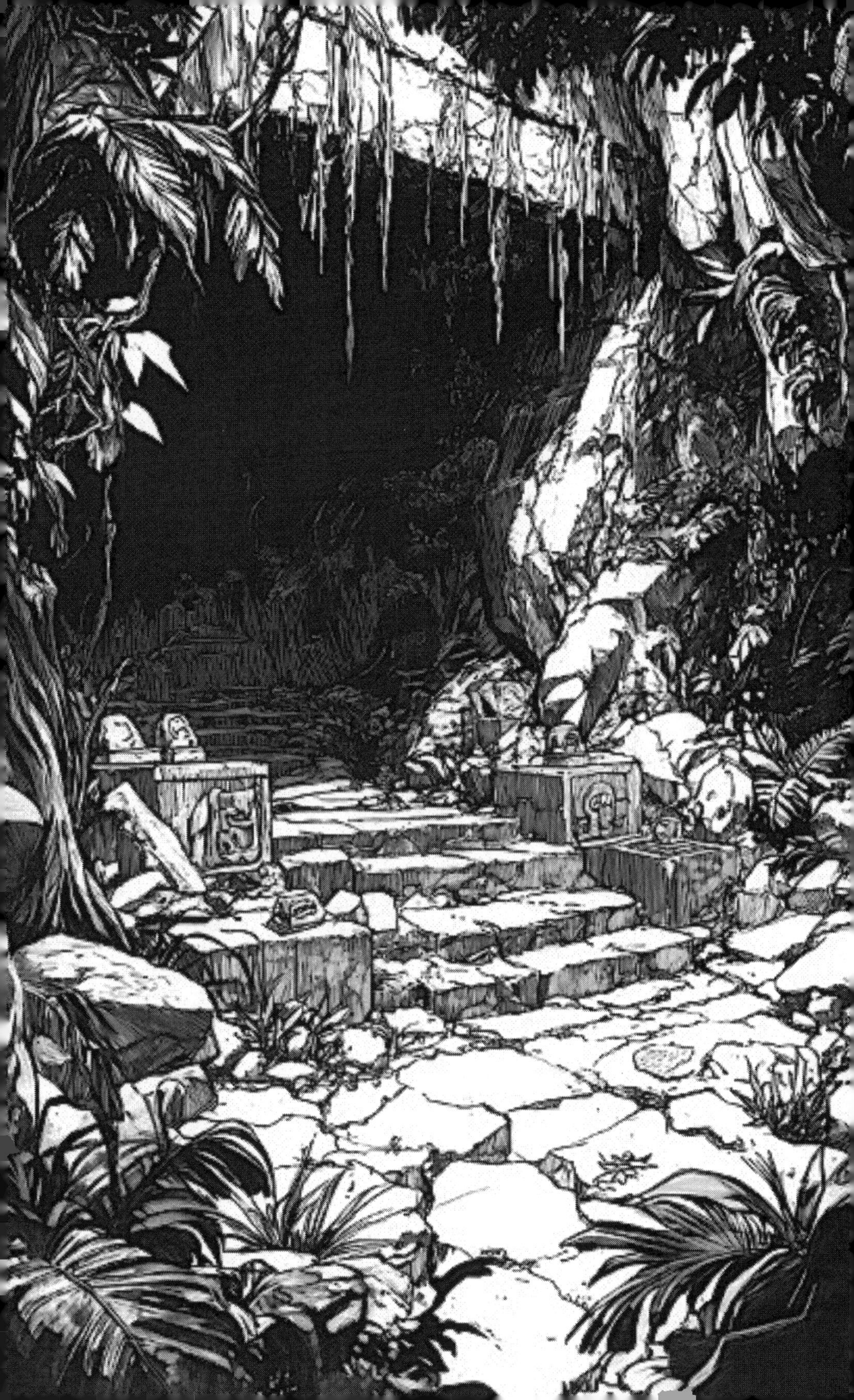

Fact 100 - Caves were seen as gateways to the beyond

For the Maya, caves were more than just natural formations. They represented portals to the underworld, a sacred place where the spirits of the dead and deities dwelt. These subterranean spaces symbolized the entrance to Xibalba, the realm of the dead, a concept deeply rooted in Mayan cosmology. The caves were believed to connect the world of the living with that of the ancestors and gods, offering a direct passageway between these realities.

Ceremonies in the caves were commonplace and involved complex rituals, often led by the most powerful priests. Offerings such as ceramics, jade, shells and even sacrifices were placed there to honor the underworld gods and appease the spirits. The darkness and humidity of the caves accentuated the mysticism of these rituals, reinforcing their sacred and mysterious character.

Some caves, like those at Balankanché, were designed to resemble underground sanctuaries. They contained altars and sculptures, transforming these natural spaces into veritable temples. The Maya also used the caves' limestone formations and stalactites as spiritual elements, associating them with divine forces. The reflections of flames on the walls, creating moving shadows, reinforced the impression of being in the presence of the spirits.

Mayan myths and legends are full of stories involving caves as access points to invisible worlds. In these stories, heroes or priests entered caves to face trials, consult the gods or seek answers to their destinies. These stories underline the importance of caves in Mayan culture, not only as physical places, but also as powerful symbols of transformation and spiritual connection.

Today, archaeological discoveries in these caves continue to reveal clues to the Maya worldview. The objects found, often well-preserved thanks to humidity and isolation, give us a unique insight into these ancient practices. They show the extent to which the Maya saw caves not only as refuges or sources of water, but above all as sacred spaces, essential to understanding their relationship with the cosmos and the afterlife.

Conclusion

After exploring these 100 Amazing Facts about the Maya, you've traveled through the history of a civilization that, despite the centuries that separate us, continues to amaze us with its complexity and grandeur. The Maya are not simply figures of the past; their legacy still resonates today, from the majestic ruins to the living traditions of their descendants. By discovering their innovations, beliefs and challenges, you've touched the soul of a people who saw the universe in a unique and inspiring way.

The Maya tamed the jungle, deciphered the sky and created a culture that celebrated the intimate connection between man, nature and the divine. Their pyramids still point to the stars, testifying to their mastery of astronomy, while their carved glyphs tell tales of gods, kings and heroes. As you read these Facts, you may have realized just how rich and multidimensional their worldview was, blending science, art and spirituality in fascinating harmony.

This journey to the heart of Mayan civilization has shown you just how advanced their knowledge and creativity were for their time. From their water management systems to their precise calendars and ritual practices, the Maya remind us that the quest for meaning and connection transcends time. Their ability to adapt to their environment, solve complex problems and celebrate life through their customs and monuments remains a source of inspiration.

As you close this book, remember that the Maya are not simply relics frozen in the past. They are present in every stone carved, every legend told, and every tradition perpetuated by their descendants. Their story is not over; it continues to evolve as we discover new knowledge about their world. Your exploration of the 100 Facts is just the beginning, an invitation to continue this adventure beyond the pages.

Whether this book has shed new light on the Maya, inspired you or simply filled you with wonder, know that the spirit of the Maya lives on in every discovery and every glimpse of their heritage. By keeping their lessons and stories alive, you too can help keep the flame of this extraordinary civilization alive. Thank you for being a fellow traveller on this odyssey to the heart of the Mayan world.

Marc Dresgui

Quiz

1) What was the approximate length of the solar year according to the Mayan calendar?

    a)   365.25 days
    b)   365.5 days
    c)   365.2420 days
    d)   365.1 days

2) What was the main function of the Mayan "sacbés" or white roads?

    a)   For war chariot racing
    b)   For transport and trade between cities
    c)   To demarcate city territories
    d)   For water purification rituals

3) What was the main use of Mayan hieroglyphs?

    a)   To decorate royal garments
    b)   To predict star movements
    c)   To record the history, beliefs and daily life of the Mayas
    d)   To create city maps

4) What symbolic role did the jaguar play in Mayan culture?

    a)   Represented fertility and harvests
    b)   embodied wisdom and knowledge
    c)   Symbolized power, royalty and the spirit world
    d)   Was associated with peace and prosperity

5) What was the main function of Mayan frescoes in their temples and palaces?

    a)   Decorate walls with geometric patterns
    b)   Telling vibrant stories of everyday life, rituals and myths
    c)   Protecting walls from the elements
    d)   Indicate agricultural and astronomical calendars

6) What was the main material used to make the shields of Mayan warriors?

    a)   Metal
    b)   Pierre
    c)   Wood
    d)   Bones

7) What was the main material used by the Maya to carve their monumental statues?

    a)   Bronze
    b)   Granite

- c) Marble
- d) Limestone

8) What was the main reason the Maya used conches as instruments?
- a) To hunt animals
- b) To create jewelry
- c) For religious ceremonies and rituals
- d) To decorate their homes

9) What irrigation techniques did the Maya use to cultivate lakes and swamps?
- a) Aqueducts
- b) Catchment wells
- c) Chinampas
- d) Water mills

10) Why were cenotes considered sacred places by the Maya?
- a) They served only as sources of drinking water.
- b) They were seen as gateways to Xibalba, the underworld.
- c) They were used to store food supplies.
- d) They were gathering places for local markets.

11) What was the main function of the various levels in Mayan cities?
- a) They were used for decorative purposes only.
- b) They were used to manage rainwater and flooding.
- c) They separated social functions and symbolized the power of the elite.
- d) They were designed to maximize sun exposure for crops.

12) What was the main function of masks in Mayan ceremonies?
- a) They were used to scare off enemies during wars.
- b) They were used to honor ancestors and invoke them during rituals.
- c) They represented the rain gods to ensure good harvests.
- d) They were worn exclusively by children during celebrations.

13) What was the main function of Mayan frescoes in temples and palaces?
- a) They were used to decorate the walls of private residences.
- b) They celebrated great military victories and the exploits of leaders.
- c) They exclusively depicted scenes from everyday life.
- d) They were used to predict astronomical events.

14) What was the symbolic function of feathers in Mayan royal costumes?
- a) They were used to represent fertility and abundance.
- b) They were used to scare off enemies in battle.
- c) They symbolized wealth, power and a link with the divine.

d) They indicated the age and experience of the warriors.

15) What was the main function of clay figurines among the Maya?
 a) They were mainly used as farming tools.
 b) They were used for games and entertainment.
 c) They represented ancient myths and served to convey mythological tales.
 d) They were used exclusively as temple decorations.

16) What was the main reason why the Maya used shell instruments in their rituals?
 a) To predict star movements.
 b) To announce the start of public procurement.
 c) To summon spirits and mark important moments in ceremonies.
 d) To measure time during rituals.

17) What role did bone flutes play in Mayan religious rituals?
 a) They were used to predict climate change.
 b) They guided the movements of priests and participants during ceremonies.
 c) They were only used for harvest festivals.
 d) They replaced drums to mark ritual time.

18) Why were mountains considered sacred by the Maya?
 a) They were used as storage sites for crops.
 b) They served as landmarks for navigating through the jungle.
 c) They embodied the connection between the earthly world and the heavens, and were home to spirits and divinities.
 d) They were only places of refuge in case of enemy attack.

19) Why were Mayan monuments often aligned with the stars?
 a) To facilitate trade between city-states.
 b) To mark important events in their calendar and connect with their gods associated with celestial bodies.
 c) To improve natural ventilation inside structures.
 d) To indicate the direction of rivers and water sources.

20) Why did the Maya consider caves to be sacred places?
 a) Because they offered safe shelter from the elements.
 b) Because they were important sources of drinking water.
 c) Because they symbolized portals to the underworld, connecting the world of the living to that of the ancestors and gods.
 d) Because they were used to store treasure and provisions in times of war.

Answers

1) What was the approximate length of the solar year according to the Mayan calendar?

Correct answer: c) 365.2420 days

2) What was the main function of the Mayan "sacbés" or white roads?

Correct answer: b) For transport and trade between cities

3) What was the main use of Mayan hieroglyphs?

Correct answer: c) To record Mayan history, beliefs and daily life.

4) What symbolic role did the jaguar play in Mayan culture?

Correct answer: c) Symbolized power, royalty and the spirit world

5) What was the main function of Mayan frescoes in their temples and palaces?

Correct answer: b) Telling vibrant stories of everyday life, rituals and myths

6) What was the main material used to make the shields of Mayan warriors?

Correct answer: c) Wood

7) What was the main material used by the Maya to carve their monumental statues?

Correct answer: d) Limestone

8) What was the main reason the Maya used conches as instruments?

Correct answer: c) For religious ceremonies and rituals

9) What irrigation techniques did the Maya use to cultivate lakes and swamps?

Correct answer: c) Chinampas

10) Why were cenotes considered sacred places by the Maya?

Correct answer: b) They were seen as gateways to Xibalba, the underworld.

11) What was the main function of the various levels in Mayan cities?

Correct answer: c) They separated social functions and symbolized the power of the elite.

12) What was the main function of masks in Mayan ceremonies?

Correct answer: b) They were used to honor ancestors and invoke them during rituals.

13) What was the main function of Mayan frescoes in temples and palaces?

Correct answer: b) They celebrated great military victories and the exploits of leaders.

14) What was the symbolic function of feathers in Mayan royal costumes?

Correct answer: c) They symbolized wealth, power and a link with the divine.

15) What was the main function of clay figurines among the Maya?

Correct answer: c) They represented ancient myths and were used to convey mythological tales.

16) What was the main reason why the Maya used shell instruments in their rituals?

Correct answer: c) To summon spirits and mark important ceremonial moments.

17) What role did bone flutes play in Mayan religious rituals?

Correct answer: b) They guided the movements of priests and participants during ceremonies.

18) Why were mountains considered sacred by the Maya?

Correct answer: c) They embodied the connection between the earthly world and the heavens, and were home to spirits and deities.

19) Why were Mayan monuments often aligned with the stars?

Correct answer: b) To mark important events in their calendar and connect with their gods associated with celestial bodies.

20) Why did the Maya consider caves to be sacred places?

Correct answer: c) Because they symbolized portals to the underworld, connecting the world of the living to that of the ancestors and gods.

Made in the USA
Middletown, DE
30 December 2024